Jean Genet

Titles in the series Critical Lives present the work of leading cultural figures of the modern period. Each book explores the life of the artist, writer, philosopher or architect in question and relates it to their major works.

In the same series

Michel Foucault
David Macey

Pablo Picasso
Mary Ann Caws

Jean Genet

Stephen Barber

REAKTION BOOKS

For J.

Published by Reaktion Books Ltd
79 Farringdon Road
London EC1M 3JU, UK

www.reaktionbooks.co.uk

First published 2004

Introduction copyright © Edmund White 2004
Main text copyright © Stephen Barber 2004

The publishers and author gratefully acknowledge support for the
publication of this book by: A·H·R·B

Printed and bound by Biddles Ltd, Kings's Lynn

British Library Cataloguing in Publication Data
Barber, Stephen, 1961 –
    Jean Genet. – (Critical lives)
    1. Genet, Jean, 1910 – 1986 2. Authors, French – 20th century –
    Biography
    I. Title
    848.9'1209

ISBN 1 86189 178 4

Contents

Introduction

Edmund White

Jean Genet's life describes an astonishingly unpredictable arc,
to which none of the usual biographical approaches is adequate.
A foundling, Genet was placed as an infant with a family in the
small town of Alligny in the heart of the Morvan, one of the
poorest areas of France. There he was raised among peasants
who spoke a dialect incomprehensible to Parisians, though
Genet himself insisted unaccountably on speaking the 'correct'
French he was taught in school. He was a brilliant scholar and
won the top local academic prize. But soon enough he ran away
from the trade school where the state had placed him at age
twelve – and from then on he was heading for a life of marginality
and sometimes petty crime.

He was confined to an infamous reform school, Mettray, where
he learned to love rough boys. Afterwards he joined the army and
was shipped out to Damascus, where he first came into contact with
the Arab world that would figure large in his writings and in his
political sympathies. He was a beggar and vagabond in Spain at the
heart of the Depression. He was arrested frequently for 'crimes' that
seldom amounted to more than stealing fabric samples or doctoring
a train ticket. He made a *hegira* across Central Europe during the
rise of Nazism and was in Berlin soon after Hitler came to power.
He was in prison several times in Paris during the Occupation, and
only the intervention of Cocteau kept him from being given a life
sentence as a multiple offender.

Genet was largely self-taught, but he was someone who haunted the bookstores (and often stole from them) and even sold books himself along the quay not far from Notre-Dame. He wrote screenplays, novels, poems and highly personal essays. His fiction is so explicitly homosexual – and erotic and transgressive – that it had to be published under the counter throughout the war years. When he finally emerged after the war as a playwright of a popular, commercially successful hit, *The Maids*, and as the novelist who had penned five extraordinarily rich and densely imagined books in just five years, he was widely acclaimed by the leading minds of the day. In fact, Genet had the rare privilege (or curse) of having a huge tome devoted to him while he was still in his forties – Jean-Paul Sartre's *Saint Genet*. Later, another philosopher, Derrida, would devote a thick volume to him, *Glas*. And in the 1970s Genet was befriended by Michel Foucault, who wrote *Discipline and Punish* while in regular contact with Genet (the end of the book is about Genet's old reform school, Mettray).

But Genet did not become assimilated into ordinary society. He continued to live among and to champion marginal people everywhere, especially those people who were despised and rejected by even the downtrodden. In his novels he had written about the homosexual subculture (and in *Our Lady of the Flowers* he had invented the drag queen for literature). In his subsequent plays he took up the emerging African nations, for example in *The Blacks* (written before those ex-colonies had gained their independence); he espoused the cause of the Algerian revolution in *The Screens* and explored the curious political interactions between the Palace and the Bordello in *The Balcony*, his greatest study of the manipulation of power through imagery.

After he wrote his plays Genet fell into a silence of two decades but he emerged from it to participate in the violent political struggles of the Palestinians and the Black Panthers. In his last book, which Stephen Barber calls *A Loving Captive*, Genet celebrated these twin causes in his strangely personal, circular and oblique manner. This book was published shortly after his death in 1986.

The various developments in such a life obviously do not flow one from another and a biographer would have to do violence to his personal legend in order to suggest a logical evolution. Genet was undoubtedly a genius to whom the usual rules of consistency do not apply. In Stephen Barber he has found a biographer who is able to slice into the flow of his complex experience in short, thematic chapters. We are not given a record of daily life and the to-ings and fro-ings of the usual minutely circumstantial 'American-style' mammoth biography. No, what Barber brings to this task is a magisterial overview of the key episodes in Genet's existence, a profound understanding of his main artistic experiments and a lively sympathy for his political loyalties. Barber, as someone who has written extensively about avant-garde artists and about the troubled life of cities in the postwar years, brings a wide general culture as well as a sense of crisis and ambiguity to the life of Genet, which from the very beginning struck observers as being as much allegory as narrative – a big life, yet the life of the only giant of the twentieth century whose work was not universal but instead extreme, idiosyncratic, unique. I relished reading this book, the conjunction of two compatible sensibilities.

1

Jack's Hotel

Jean Genet died in the early morning hours of 15 April 1986, alone, in a room at Jack's Hotel in the avenue Stéphen Pichon: a silent, tree-lined street of no importance in Paris, suddenly cast into glory as the final site of Genet's life in the city he had endlessly transformed and reviled. All of Genet's work had been saturated in a vast obsession with death, with provoking and inventing and glorifying and dismissing death – with assembling languages and images of death, into a unique book of death. Genet's own death, intimately anticipated, still caught him violently by surprise. And that surprise of death struck Genet's readers too, since almost all had assumed him already dead after a silence of many years: Genet's death contrarily resuscitated him.

Genet had travelled to Paris earlier that month, after a journey through Spain and Morocco with his companion, Jacky Maglia. For years, he had suffered from throat cancer that weakened his body, dissolving the form of his face into a dense network of lines and void spaces which the artist Alberto Giacometti had already captured in his paintings of Genet, thirty years before. In the final photographs of Genet, his body had collapsed in on itself, reduced to an absence clothed in thick sweaters and scarves, surmounted by a head still lividly or wryly animated, but blurred by its movement into death. On his arrival in Paris, in April 1986, Genet headed for the hotel in which he habitually stayed: the Hotel Rubens, an anonymous cheap hotel in the rue du Banquier – a street that ran from nowhere to nowhere – in the Place d'Italie district of the city. But the hotel was full, and the receptionist castigated Genet for not reserving a room in advance. Jacky Maglia had to scour the surrounding streets for another hotel room for Genet. After he had located a room at the nearby Jack's Hotel, the exhausted Genet made his last journey on foot through the streets of Paris. He ascended the rue Rubens, with its vast concrete tenement blocks that housed the city's detritus: its poverty-stricken inhabitants, many of them from France's former colonial possessions. After crossing the busy boulevard de l'Hôpital, which ran down into the centre of the city, Genet had to rest on the benches outside the School of Arts and Crafts – an institution similar to the Ecole Alembert, where Genet had been sent as a thirteen-year-old boy to learn the skills of typography and from where he fled on the first of the wild excursions that would lead to his incarcerations in the children's prison of the Petite-Roquette and at the reformatory of Mettray. Genet then continued along the rue Edouard Manet, one side of which held the vaulted workshops of the School of Arts and Crafts, while the other housed the offices of the National Federation of Former Soldiers in Algeria, Tunisia and Morocco – the colonial conflicts that had seen France's national power disintegrate into the spectacles of uproar and massacre which Genet had visualized in his play *The Screens* (whose performances in Paris, in 1966, had been disrupted by rioting former soldiers of the Algerian conflict). Turning into the avenue Stéphen Pichon, Genet completed his final trajectory through the city he had outraged, perverted and insulted for more than forty years.

In his bare room at Jack's Hotel, with its telephone attached to the wall and its tiny annex for the toilet and shower cubicle, Genet lay in bed reading through the final publisher's proofs of his book, *A Loving Captive* – an immense accumulation of fragments of memory, evoking Genet's time in the Palestinian refugee camps and with the Black Panther party in the United States – which would be

Jack's Hotel, Paris, where Genet died in 1986.

published in the following month, breaking decades of near-silence. Several of Genet's friends visited him, and Jacky Maglia appeared each morning to join him for breakfast; but he was already dying. On that early morning of 15 April, he got out of bed, to urinate; terminally exhausted and weakened, he fell on the step that led to the toilet cubicle, twisted and smashed the back of his head on the tiles. Genet's death seized him in an instant. Jacky Maglia found his body in the morning. His death was notified to the municipal authorities in the Place d'Italie. On the next day, the television images and newspaper photographs showed the indifferent facade of Jack's Hotel. But Jean Genet had vanished.

The Tarnier Clinic, Paris, where Genet was born in 1910.

2

Jean Genet, the Bastard

Genet's movement across time, space, memory and oblivion had been vast and intensive over the course of his life. But, in geographical terms, he had not gone far. Seventy-six years before his sudden death at Jack's Hotel, and a mile or so to the west, his birth had been an equally unwelcome event for the proprietors of its location: the Tarnier Clinic for unmarried women, at 89 rue d'Assas, close to the Luxembourg Gardens. Genet was born there on 19 December 1910. His mother had entered the hospital – a charity clinic run by the Public Assistance authorities – over a month earlier. She took her child, registered as having an unknown father, back to her room in the rue Broca. But, during the following summer, she definitively abandoned her child Jean to the authorities; from the moment that she handed over the infant to the 'Bureau d'Abandon' she lost all power and rights over her child (all that remained was her continuing right to have confirmed whether Jean was alive or dead). Jean Genet, until he reached adulthood, had become the responsibility and property of the French state, to dispose of as it saw fit.

Genet's work is constellated with images of the Mother – who can capriciously change sexes, become black or white, a child or a silent old woman; in his final book, *A Loving Captive*, he searches for a transient but permanent and omniscient mother in the form of an elderly Palestinian who had watched over him for one night, over a decade earlier, enacting for Genet the gestures she ordinarily performed for her own son, a fighter absent on a mission of death. In all of Genet's mothers, the human form flickers and blacks out, blurring into death. The mother is unknown. Camille Gabrielle Genet died during the great, Europe-wide influenza epidemic of 1918–19; but Genet knew nothing of her death – his case-file remained closed to him, even in adulthood, and he heard only fragments of his own origins (his mother's first names, the unknown status of his father) during his subsequent trials and sentencings. He had not only been cast into the world as an unwanted bastard, but the language used to identify, castigate and imprison him, on the authority of the French state, was rendered through his mother's abandonment and refusal of him. Genet would be permanently wounded by the mystery of his mother: in his childhood he was obsessed to know why she had abandoned him, and later in life he would dismiss or experience anger at his own mother, instead proliferating new mothers for himself and generating his own, self-contained genealogy and origins. Genet's mother may or may not have been a prostitute; in documents, she defined herself as a 'maidservant' or 'governess'. Genet himself could seize the unknown space between identities or fixed definitions for his own work: as a revolutionary, a homosexual, a novelist, a traveller, a film maker, a criminal, a playwright: simultaneously incandescent in his multiple creativity, and a blank, elusive presence. Of Genet's father, no trace was ever found.

The surrendering of the infant Genet to the French state made him a captive of that power from the age of seven months; even the arrangement of the unmarried mothers' beds in the Tarnier clinic had resembled a carceral system of cells under surveillance, and Genet's first seven months with his mother in Paris, certainly in poverty and desperation, became a provisional release before he was irreparably drawn back into the domain of the Public Assistance. Genet's virulent hatred of the French authorities – and of France itself, and of its language, against and in which he would create his own language – began at the moment of his birth. But it would be a necessary, lifelong hatred: inflected contrarily with rapidly cancelled traces of love and tenderness, and pursued often from a distance from France, in exile in North Africa, Greece, Japan and the Middle East.

Once Genet had been abandoned to the Public Assistance authorities, on 28 July 1911, his disposal for adoption and dispatch to foster parents in the rural Morvan region was executed with supreme speed (the same process had been at work for unwanted children in Paris since the seventeenth century). Only two days later, he had been taken by train to the town of Saulieu, over a hundred miles to the south-east of Paris, and handed over to the Regnier family in the village of Alligny-en-Morvan. Genet would not return to Paris for another fourteen years.

3

The Criminal Child

The Morvan was an isolated land – the 'black country' in the name's Celtic origin – without industry and with only harsh farming of the barren earth. The men of the region were renowned for their devotion to alcohol. But the Morvan also had the reputation for the warmth of its inhabitants to strangers, and the Public Assistance authorities in Paris had been sending abandoned children to families there for many decades. The families were intended to raise the children with religious rigour, and in return received regular sums of money, which formed a primary income for the region's poverty-stricken inhabitants. At the time Genet was in the Morvan, he was one of several thousand Public Assistance children being housed there – most of whom never returned to Paris but spent their lives as itinerant farmworkers. Genet had the exceptional fortune to be allocated to a family that cared for him and whose house was one of the largest in the village of Alligny; other Public Assistance children in Alligny during Genet's time there, such as Louis Cullaffroy and Jean Querelle – whose names he would appropriate for the principal characters in two of his novels of the 1940s – were brutally treated, set apart from the families housing them and used as slave labour. Genet was given a room of his own and left to daydream and explore the surrounding countryside as he grew up; his foster parents, Charles and Eugénie Regnier, ran a carpentry workshop and tobacco shop in the house. At school, Genet and the other Public Assistance children were invisibly separated out from the village children; Genet was also distinguished by his self-imposed distance from all of his companions, by his intelligence (he was one of the very few children to pass the Certificate of Studies examination) and by his already-evident capacity for theft – by the age of ten, he was already stealing small items around the village, although this ceased when his foster mother suddenly died in 1922 and he was transferred to the care of her daughter. In his final year in Alligny, from the age of thirteen to fourteen, Genet was given a single duty by his foster family: each day he took the family's one cow out to a field beyond the village, spent the day there and returned with the cow in the evening.

The great distraction and entertainment for the inhabitants of Alligny during those years was the regular arrival of a travelling cinema, which set up its screen in the centre of the village for several days at a time and projected its silent films (accompanied by shouted explanations and music) in the darkness to the entranced, awestruck peasants, who saw fabulous images of cities and of part-naked human bodies for the first time. The travelling cinema became the seminal impulse behind Genet's own cinema projects, and also one of the irrepressible forces that generated his constant flights and escapes of the next years.

At the age of thirteen, Genet was sent to an arts and crafts school outside Paris, the Ecole Alembert, to learn the profession of typography; the Public Assistance authorities accorded him this rare opportunity (most abandoned children were simply left in the Morvan) because of his success in the Certificate of Studies examination. But, almost immediately, Genet fled from the Ecole Alembert – he was the only escapee in that year, 1924 – and was arrested in Nice, where he claimed to be on his way to the United States or Egypt to realize his cinema ambitions. Very rapidly, his renunciation of taking on a profession was rendering his aspirations as criminal. The Public Assistance authorities tried again with Genet, allocating him to a celebrated composer of maudlin popular songs, René de Buxeuil, to serve as his assistant; René de Buxeuil was blind and in need of someone to help him through the streets of Paris. But after several months, Genet disappeared again with some money entrusted to him, and spent it at a fairground; dismissed by René de Buxeuil, he had transformed himself in the space of a year from a prestigious success of the Public Assistance to a scandalous, criminal child. He was sent to the Henri-Rousselle clinic at the Sainte-Anne mental hospital for a psychiatric report to be compiled, and was diagnosed as suffering from a degree of 'mental weakness'. Wherever he was placed, he fled; but his lack of resources to carry through his ambitions and obsessions meant that he was repeatedly arrested, ticket-less, on trains heading for ports. In March 1926, at the age of fifteen, he was sent to the Petite-Roquette prison in eastern Paris; built as a panopticon in the 1830s, the Petite-Roquette held children from the age of six upwards in total silence and isolation from one another. At its construction, it had been seen as a revolutionary medium of incarceration for the purification of criminal children, but it was now near-derelict (it would later serve as a women's prison and as a detention centre for Resistance fighters during the German Occupation of Paris, before its demolition in 1974); Genet spent three months in one of the Petite-Roquette cells, the walls painted black to their mid-point, then white to the ceiling. On his release, he continued his flights and train arrests; but he had already accumulated an aura of near-irreparable criminality that had cancelled out the scholarly promise he had manifested in the Morvan. After a final arrest in July 1926, Genet was condemned to the agricultural penal colony of Mettray.

The Petite-Roquette Prison in Paris, where Genet was imprisoned at the age of fifteen in 1926.

4

The Mettray Colony

The Mettray prison colony – in the Touraine region, to the south-
west of Paris – with its population of punitively disciplined youths,
formed a sexually charged Eden for Genet, both during his stay
and for the rest of his life. He had his first sexual experiences there,
and the isolated, self-sufficient world of Mettray possessed all of
the forces of aberration and perversion that exhilarated him.
Above all, it was a prison without walls, its pavilions surrounded
by flowers and open countryside. As an old man, Genet noted:
'One of the finest inventions of the Colony of Mettray was to have
known not to put a wall around it . . . It's much more difficult to
escape when you have to cross a bed of flowers.'[1] Although Mettray
had appeared a radical and prestigious experiment on its opening
in the 1840s (in the same way that the Petite-Roquette children's
prison had seemed innovative in form to its instigators), it had fallen
into near-dereliction by the time Genet spent his three years there;
the buildings were rapidly deteriorating, the colony's staff no
longer possessed the mission of rehabilitation of their original
predecessors, and Mettray was deeply in debt as an institution during
Genet's time there. He was being incarcerated in a penal system
whose grandiose intentions of the previous century had entirely
evanesced, so that Genet passed through the ghosts and broken
fragments of prisons rather than being held in stasis by their once-
monumental forms; that dereliction of Mettray enabled Genet to
overlayer it with his volatile preoccupations and sexually to re-
create it in his novels and film projects. Mettray continued to fall

Genet in an institution for young offenders at Mettray, 1927.

apart in the decade after Genet had left, finally closing down as a penal colony in 1939.

The founders of Mettray had intended to reconfigure the salutary form of the family in each of the colony's pavilions, as an all-male hierarchy with absolute power and discipline. Every act of forced labour and brutal punishment was inflected by religion – the day was punctuated by regular prayer sessions, and the severest punishments involved depositing the youths in freezing, suffocating cells, in a near-darkness within which they could perceive only the large white letters on their cell wall: 'God sees you'. Many prisoners of the cells froze to death. The harshest retribution was allocated on the discovery of sodomy or masturbation among the youths, who spent much of their time walking endlessly in circles under the watchful eye of the family's 'older brother'. The youths were given gruelling manual work to do in the fields surrounding the colony and in its workshops. In order to leave the colony, most of them signed up for long periods of army service at an office located on the site; Mettray had a tradition of training its prisoners for the navy, but, by Genet's time there, the navy had stopped recruiting the subjugated, uneducated Mettray colonists. The institution's reputation was in freefall, with the onset of the journalism campaigns denouncing Mettray's regime that would contribute to its closure.

Genet's years at Mettray, as a shaven-headed and uniformed prisoner working long hours planting vegetables and making brushes, were as tortuous and unrelenting as those of all the prisoners; he made one attempt at escape, on 3 December 1927, heading from Mettray towards the capital on foot, and was soon recaptured and severely punished. But the nights at Mettray supplanted the inept, arcane discipline of the day with sexual celebrations of cruelty, violence and ecstasy among the youths in each pavilion, who instigated intricate hierarchies of lust and loyalty that negated the punitive hierarchies deployed by the colony's governors and wardens. Genet himself passed through that capricious sexual regime, from the role of uninitiated novice to seasoned veteran, his prestige enhanced after his escape attempt. The seething corporeal forces of sex and subdued rebellion (each projected by an urgent sensory language between the young inmates) would remain a primary obsession for Genet throughout his life. Only Genet lauded the memory of Mettray in all of the accounts of the colony after its closure, provocatively sanctifying its abjections and sexual furores while denouncing the desire for wealth that lay at the origin of the colony's creation. The criminal youths of Mettray would become the population of France's adult prisons, where Genet would meet them again. Although in later life he transformed his years at Mettray, lovingly and expansively, Genet – like all of the colony's inhabitants – had been eager to leave at the first possible opportunity. On 1 March 1929, at the age of eighteen, he entered the army recruitment office and enlisted for two years' military service.

5

Crossings of Europe

Genet spent almost seven years of his life as a soldier, from his enlistment at Mettray until his desertion on 18 June 1936, interspersed with short periods of civilian life. But they were years which Genet later preferred to cast into oblivion; he concertinaed them in his writings and interviews, so that his time as a French soldier appeared compacted into a few months rather than seven years. Genet never advanced in rank in the army and never fought in any conflicts; he presented it as a time of passivity, in which he subjugated himself to the orders he received and ceased to think. Although most of Genet's time as a soldier was spent in the barracks towns of Provence, he was also sent to countries in which France was attempting to consolidate its colonial power: to Syria in 1929, where Genet witnessed the decimated ruins of Damascus (which had been destroyed by the French army to subdue an uprising), and to Morocco in 1931. The only fragment of memory which Genet ever extracted in later life from the oblivion of his military years was a story told in his final book, *A Loving Captive*, of how he had been assigned the responsibility, in Damascus, of commanding the construction of a tower on which a cannon was to be placed; neither Genet nor his workmen had any idea how to build a tower, but they improvised its construction and the cannon was placed at its summit. When the cannon was fired for the first time, to celebrate the tower's construction, Genet's work came undone: the impact fissured the concrete tower into a spider's web of flaws, and it ignominiously collapsed to the ground. Genet remembered: 'I was repatriated to France and given a month's convalescence, but my military career was shattered.'[2]

Genet's desertion from the army in 1936 added another dimension of criminality to his already multiply-castigated and condemned life; he had been transferred to an elite colonial regiment whose severe discipline and preparation for combat were alien to the passive stasis Genet had grown accustomed to in his military existence. He acquired a passport and altered the name with a few adept gestures, transforming 'Genet' to 'Gejietti' in order to avoid being apprehended for his desertion. Genet then began a vast journey, compulsively crossing and re-crossing Europe from July 1936 to July 1937, in total poverty, always travelling by foot and in perpetual danger of being arrested as a vagabond and expelled from the country he was travelling through. His hair grew down to his shoulders as he moved from city to city, scanning the disintegrating countries of Europe as they headed into warfare.

From his barracks in Aix-en-Provence, Genet travelled to Nice and through Italy to the southern port of Brindisi (as with his very first flight, from the Ecole Alembert in 1924, Genet almost always headed south, as though that were the direction of glory); he crossed the Adriatic to Albania and reached its capital, Tiranë, but was arrested there and ordered to leave. After unsuccessfully attempting to cross from the port of Sarandë to Corfu (where the Greek police refused him entry), Genet headed north into Yugoslavia. In Belgrade, he was arrested as a suspected spy and held for a month in the town of Užižka-Požega before being expelled back to Italy. From Trieste, near the Yugoslavian border, he traversed the entire country, south to Sicily, before being arrested in Palermo and deported north to Austria. He reached Vienna but was expelled again; his journey incessantly and grudgingly crossed frontiers, as though negating them and their power. He arrived in the Czech city of Brno at the end of 1936 and was arrested again;

Genet's identity card photograph, *c.* 1937.

however, instead of deporting him, the Czech authorities assigned Genet into the care of a philanthropic organization, the League for Human Rights. He stayed with a German refugee family, the Pringsheims, and slept on the exterior balcony of their (now-demolished) apartment in the suburb of Bohunice, on the south-western periphery of the city; one of the daughters of the family later remembered that the genial Genet always wore a black roll-neck pullover under a chestnut-coloured corduroy suit, and never took them off. Genet made a little money giving French lessons to the wife of a German industrialist, Ann Bloch, during his five months in Brno before heading north to Poland – to Kraków and Katowice. Arrested and expelled yet again, he travelled north-west to Germany, to Berlin, where he witnessed the impact of Hitler's power. For Genet, who spent his time taking walks by the river Spree in his elegant destitution, Berlin had fallen apart; over forty years later, he evoked the city of 1937 to the German film producer Dieter Schidor: 'Berlin was like a third-world city. Everyone there was emaciated – except for Göring.'[3] Finally, in July 1937, Genet travelled to Paris, though the momentum of his journeys was still strong, and he was formulating new travels, to Africa and America; but in Paris, Genet's life abruptly changed – from the perpetual movement of his journeys, he now became enmeshed in a new existence of imprisonment and of writing.

6

Genet's Prisons

Genet's career in the prisons of France lasted for around seven years, like his career as a soldier – but whereas his military life left virtually no trace whatsoever on his writings, Genet's prison years provided the raw material, almost always transformed and glorified, for his novels, film projects and theatre. And it was in three of his prisons, the Santé and the Camp des Tourelles in Paris and Fresnes in the city's periphery, that Genet wrote his first two novels, *Our Lady of the Flowers* and *Miracle of the Rose*. Just as Genet manipulated the time and space of his own early life (expanding the year of his crossings of Europe, contracting his years of military life), he would also reinvent his crimes, both in his novels written in prison and in his later interviews; all of Genet's imprisonments came from momentary acts of petty theft, rather than from the intensively pursued life of burglary, with its intimations of violence and murder, that Genet evoked.

Genet's first arrest took place in September 1937, two months after his return to Paris from his journeys – he was caught stealing handkerchiefs in the Samaritaine department store (while an accomplice diverted the shop assistants' attention), but was released as a 'first offender'. Only three days later, on 21 September, the police chased Genet along the rue des Couronnes in the east of Paris and caught him at the junction with the rue Vilin; this time, he was arrested for stealing from cars and for carrying a gun, and sent to the Santé and then to Fresnes prison. From his doctored

The Santé Prison, Paris, where Genet was imprisoned several times between 1937 and 1943, and which formed a key site of his fiction.

identity papers, the police discovered Genet's identity as a military deserter from the previous year, and he was sent to Marseilles to be judged by a military tribunal; although the medical examinations he underwent there detected 'instability' and 'immorality', Genet was given a light sentence. Despite now being forbidden from re-joining the army, Genet headed for the north-western port of Brest and signed up for service with a colonial regiment, but was soon arrested for stealing bottles of spirits from a shop in Brest and imprisoned there. Back in Paris after his release, Genet became a fixture at the Brasserie Graff in the place Blanche, in Montmartre, offering criminal services to the clients; but his own crimes were petty and ludicrously opportunistic – one of his specialities at this time was to try on a suit in a tailor's shop and then run off at high speed without paying for it. Although Genet was very poor in the short intervals between his prison stays, he always appeared suave in appearance; after being arrested for travelling by train using a forged ticket, Genet was described by a local newspaper: 'Elegantly dressed, his flat face topped by wavy brown hair, with hollow eyes and a turned-up nose . . . '.[4] After more arrests in Paris's depart-ment stores, Genet was dispatched to Fresnes, re-emerging in Paris on 14 June 1940: the very same day that the invading German troops arrived to occupy the silent, near-deserted city. Genet remembered: 'I was happy . . . Yes, the French were cowardly.'[5] A large part of the population had fled.

Under the German Occupation, Genet's thefts in Paris and imprisonments continued relentlessly; the only difference was that he was now stealing books rather than suits and linen; after being arrested for book theft on 3 December 1940, he joked at his trial that he was attempting to improve his education through his thefts, and that he always surreptitiously returned the books he had stolen. He met a young Trotskyite student named Jean Decarnin and together they developed a market in stolen and re-sold books; Decarnin worked at a quayside bookstall by the Notre-Dame

cathedral, and Genet himself sometimes looked after the stall
when not in prison. The only variation in his imprisonments
for book thefts came in December 1941, when he was chased by
the police after stealing three metres of cloth from a tailor, and
captured on the southern end of the Notre-Dame bridge. Genet's
repeated convictions meant that he was examined on two occa-
sions to assess the possibility of sending him to a lunatic asylum; he
was also in danger of being sentenced to life imprisonment from
the accumulated number of his convictions. And the German
Occupation of Paris brought its own, unpredictable dangers. After
an arrest for book-theft in June 1943, he had to declare: 'I am a
bachelor, of French nationality. Not a Jew.'[6] Dispatched to the
Santé, he was then transferred to the Camp des Tourelles, a vast
collection of detention buildings and soldiers' barracks on the eastern
edge of Paris; the prison, run by the French militia in collaboration
with the German police, was being used as a centre for the round-
ing-up of Resistance fighters and political prisoners before their
transferral to the German concentration camps. (The grim prison
still stands in Paris, heavily guarded as a 'military zone' and still
carrying warning signs from Genet's time there: 'It is forbidden to
film and to photograph'.) On 24 September 1943, Genet was arrested
for the last time, again for book-theft; again, he passed through the
Santé and was transferred to the Camp des Tourelles. An emer-
gency public security law issued by the German authorities rendered
all criminals without a home or profession, such as Genet, liable
now to permanent detention; although Genet's last conviction had
been for only four months, he now entered a precarious and potentially lethal zone where he was himself in imminent danger of
being included in a shipment of prisoners to a concentration camp.
He desperately tried to formulate a way to get out of the Camp des
Tourelles, pleading for his friends to help him and contemplating an
escape attempt that would have resulted in his being fired-upon
by the heavily-armed guards. But on 19 March 1944, five months

before the end of the German Occupation, Genet was abruptly freed from the Camp des Tourelles. The repercussions of his imprisonments continued to hang over him for many years; in 1951, he was questioned by the police about the non-payment of a large fine left over from a conviction from 1940 (when Genet had been sentenced in his absence for one crime while already imprisoned for another), and had urgently to find the money for the fine in order not to return to prison. But in March 1944, on his exit from the Camp des Tourelles, Genet had spent his last moment in prison.

7

Our Lady of the Flowers

Genet's *Our Lady of the Flowers* constitutes the most incendiary and original first novel of the twentieth century: its impact transformed sexual culture worldwide, suffusing such events as the New York Stonewall gay liberation uprising of 1969, the Tokyo street riots of the same period (for which Genet's work provided the inspiration of a revolutionary culture of violence adhered by deviant, dissident sexuality), and innumerable works in art, film, dance and writing for which Genet's novel formed an irresistible inspiration to propel images and languages to their most challenging or extreme boundaries. But Genet's novel is written in a language of supreme seduction and pure mystery, its raw material of sex acts, crimes and death projected in an enveloping medium of ocular and sensory captivations: it appeared out of nowhere, traceable to some degree in Genet's extended readings and film-viewings (from childhood, from his army years and travels) of Rimbaud, Proust and gangster-film melodramas, but simultaneously without origin or precedent. *Our Lady of the Flowers* was written in 1942, principally during Genet's imprisonment for theft at the Fresnes gaol; Genet wrote on whatever paper came to hand in prison, on paper sacks and rough notebooks, usually sitting on the edge of his bed with the thick paper positioned on his knees. In later years, Genet would often recount that the first fifty or so pages of *Our Lady of the Flowers* had been confiscated and destroyed by the prison authorities on their discovery by a guard while Genet was out in the exercise yard – he had had to launch immediately back to the beginning, piecing together the vivid and hallucinated fragments of language from memory; but Genet's story of the manuscript's destruction was a fabrication or mis-remembering, since it was actually the initial part of his subsequent novel, *Miracle of the Rose*, that was confiscated.

Genet invented the figure of the drag queen for art and literature in *Our Lady of the Flowers*, in a language that veers wildly from splendour to obscenity, from argot to elegy. At the novel's opening, its principal character, the drag-queen prostitute Divine, is already dead from tuberculosis: the narrative proceeds by aberrant flashbacks, moving at capricious will through time and space (including that of the very-present Genet's imagining and writing of the book) as it traces Divine's ascent to glory in the alleys and bars of Montmartre, from his origin as the child Lou Culafroy in a backward rural village. The three interlocked spaces of the novel are the prison cell in which Genet announces that he is creating his fictional world (most immediately to saturate himself within, for his sessions of masturbation in solitude); the teeming streets of Montmartre with their population entirely consisting of vitriolic drag queens, handsome pimps with enormous penises, and hierarchically preoccupied criminals living ephemeral, charged moments between prison spells; and, finally, the space of Divine's attic room, marooned far above Paris and looking down on the Montmartre cemetery. Divine's narrative is meshed with that of one of his young criminal lovers, dubbed Our Lady of the Flowers, who is in a suspended moment of survival between committing a murder and being arrested, then guillotined; that moment of survival is dense with insolent, intensive sex acts, evoked by Genet with a precision and corporeality unknown in literature at that time. Our Lady of the Flowers is walking into death, haunted and inhabited by the moments following his murdering of a lascivious old man:

'The street. Life is no longer vile. Lightheaded, he runs to a small hotel, a hotel of prostitution, and takes a room. There, to lull him, is the real night, the night of stars appearing little by little, as horror agitates his heart: it's the physical disgust of the first hour, of the murderer for the murdered – which many men have told me of. It haunts you, doesn't it? Death is active. Your death is in you; mixed into your blood, it runs in your veins, seeps from your pores, and your heart lives from death, just as a cemetery's flowers are nourished by the corpses . . . It is transmitted by your eyes, your ears, your mouth.'[7]

In *Our Lady of the Flowers*, every character's acts are inflected both by ecstasy and the presence of death, from the rampaging trajectories of the Montmartre drag queens through their night territory to Divine's memories of his incarceration as a criminal child. All languages and sensations are inscribed directly on the body in Genet's world, most tangibly in the tattooing with ink of the children in the young Divine's prison:

'All of the grimacing blue on white skin imparts a strange but powerful prestige to the child who is covered with it, like an indifferent and pure column that becomes sacred through the hieroglyphs cut into it. Sometimes, their eyelids are marked, or the armpits, the groin, the buttocks, the penis, even the soles of the feet. The signs are barbarous, full of meaning as the most barbarous signs are: maxims, bows, pierced hearts dripping with blood, faces pressed one on another, stars, crescent moons, marks, arrows, swallows, serpents, boats, triangular daggers, and inscriptions, mottos, warnings: all of it a prophetic and terrible literature.'[8]

Genet had no conception of *Our Lady of the Flowers* being published while he was writing it; it was conceived with absolute freedom, for himself alone. When it unexpectedly began to appear feasible for it to be published (initially as a clandestine edition, to escape censorship), he was resistant; he first opposed its publication altogether, then ambivalently agreed to its being published as pornography for collectors. The book would not appear in a widely-available edition for several years. Just as the world had to tense itself for the impact of Genet's language, Genet himself had to habituate himself to his exposure to the world.

8

Miracle of the Rose

Genet's second novel, *Miracle of the Rose*, was the last to be written
in prison; all of his subsequent novels would be written in hotel
rooms. Genet chose a spectacular and sombre location for the set-
ting of the novel: the medieval royal abbey of Fontevrault, in the
Touraine region to the south-west of Paris. In *Miracle of the Rose*,
Fontevrault has been transformed into a prison in which the
novel's action is set and within which Genet himself is imprisoned
as he narrates the novel. He also positions Fontevrault in intimate
proximity to the location of the Mettray reformatory, so that he
tightly binds together dual preoccupations with his memory of
Mettray (where almost all of the novel's principal characters were
interned as youths before, as adults, reaching Fontevrault) and
with the immediacy of Fontevrault, with its dense intersections of
desire and violence between the prisoners whose existence remains
inflected by the magisterial solitude and silence of the monks who
previously inhabited the cells. However, Genet was never a prisoner at Fontevrault (he visited the abbey, which was used as a prison
until the 1960s, as a tourist during the first months after his release
from the Camp des Tourelles, when the novel had already been
completed), and he geographically contracts the actual distance
between Mettray and Fontevrault to place the reformatory in the
glorious shadow of the prison. *Miracle of the Rose* was written mostly
at the prisons of Fresnes and the Santé, but was completed at the
Camp des Tourelles at the moment in February 1944 when Genet

was in greatest danger of being dispatched to a concentration camp; in conditions of extreme noise, with thirty prisoners crammed into each cell, Genet wrote the novel in thick notebooks positioned on his knees.

Miracle of the Rose explores the vast movements of memory and sensory turbulence experienced by Genet (both as the narrator of the novel and as his own character, 'Jean Genet') as his isolation expands across time, cohered only by sexual obsession and by the abrupt moments when Genet is disgorged into the communal spaces of the abbey – its stone stairwells and darkened corridors – where he ignites his relationships with other prisoners, always originating them in shared experiences of Mettray. Genet's two relationships, conducted in dense bursts of corporeal contact and expectorated whispers, are both with former inhabitants of Mettray: Divers (whose authoritarian sexual subjugation of him at the reformatory is lovingly remembered by Genet) and Bulkaen. And positioned above all of the abbey's inhabitants, the figure of Harcamone – sentenced to death for murder and awaiting execution – forms a deified, ultimately austere, presence whose origins are also those of a former Mettray prisoner: the timescale of *Miracle of the Rose* coincides with the interval of weeks between Genet's arrival at Fontevrault and Harcamone's execution, but it is also an infinitely overlayered and awry span of time, capable of insurging in any temporal direction. Its only immovable point is Genet's cell, which holds his own, aberrantly self-created freedoms:

'Now, I was a man, a liberated man. The kids and the solid-shouldered pimps, all of the children of misfortune with their bitter-tasting mouths and terrible eyes, were no longer of any use to me. I was alone. Everything is absent in prisons: even solitude.'[9]

Although Fontevrault is repopulated by Genet with his adored and insolent prisoners, all consumed in projects of violence and lust, those heated and reinforced bodies occasionally evanesce in *Miracle of the Rose* to reveal the actual anatomical form of prisoners in the Occupation-era gaols and transit camps of France: skeletally emaciated and preoccupied solely with hunger (the hallucinatory texture of the novel is itself imbued with Genet's own hunger during its writing). Everything is moving into, or already cancelled by, death: Harcamone is duly executed and Bulkaen shot down during an escape attempt. Even Genet's pivotal memory of Mettray is disintegrating, incorporated into a vision of its now-abandoned and moribund form:

'When I saw the Colony again, grass had grown between the stones, thorns and leaves penetrated through the windows that had been traversed by so many colonists, with their thighs at an angle to their bodies. The windowpanes were broken, swallows nested in the building's interior and the dark, hidden stairway, which allowed us to exchange so many kisses and caresses, had collapsed. Nothing would ever heal the sadness of my soul after looking over those ruins. I walked on quietly and heard nothing but a few birds' cries. I had found nothing but a corpse. I know that my childhood is dead.'[10]

In *Miracle of the Rose*, Genet awaits only the miraculous act (generated solely from his own imagination or compulsions) which negates and metamorphoses reality, such as the apparition of the rose which Genet snatches from Harcamone's handcuffs as he is led from his death cell. Genet's own release from the Camp des Tourelles in March 1944 itself possessed an aura of tainted miraculousness – although his friends and publishers had been attempting to secure his release, it appears to have been the intervention of a friend in intimate complicity with the prison's brutal authorities, François Sentein, that led to Genet's sudden release into Paris.

Although, in later decades, Genet would suggest that all of his five novels had been written in prison (and were written as a strategy solely to secure his liberation), he would never return to gaol: *Miracle of the Rose* was the last of Genet's writings undertaken in incarceration. In many ways, the conditions in which he created his future work would be still more exacting.

9

Genet in Occupied Paris

Genet witnessed both the Fall of Paris in 1940, with the city hastily vacated by its fleeing population, and the Liberation of Paris in 1944, with its acts of resistance against the now desperate German troops trapped in the city, together with their despised allies in the French militias. At the moment of Genet's release from the Camp des Tourelles, it was becoming clear that the Germans were going to lose the war and that the city would be retaken by the American or British forces. Until that time, the population of Paris had largely subjugated itself to, or actively colluded with, the German occupiers; sporadic outbursts of resistance had been brutally suppressed, with the tortured perpetrators either shot on the spot, dispatched to concentration camps, or interned in such prisons as the Camp des Tourelles or the Petite-Roquette. Other members of Paris's population simply adopted a stance of oblivion towards the Occupation and the pervasive presence of the German forces (who thoroughly overhauled the signs and facades of the city); retreating into internal exile and pretending that everything was functioning as normal enabled the city's inhabitants to screen themselves from the excoriating impact of the German forces on Paris. Within these dynamics of complicity, resistance and oblivion, Genet's own response to the Occupation was unique. He had been exhilarated at the city's fall, delighted both by the abject cowardice he perceived in the population (and military forces) in headlong flight, and by the abrupt cancellation of the judicial, penal and linguistic systems which had condemned him (although these would be rapidly reinstated in an amended, fascistic form which the French police authorities, in particular, wholeheartedly embraced). The emptied, silent Paris of 1940 had also been a thief's paradise for Genet. And having travelled on foot through Hitler's Germany in 1937, he knew what to expect once the Germans occupied the city. He formed sexual relationships with members of the German occupying forces, and many of his French friends both during that time and after the war (such as his lover of the late 1940s, André Babkine) would be those who had been complicit with or had actively fought for the Germans. Genet loved treachery and cowardice as forces that fractured the system he detested. But he was utterly unaligned with fascism, except for its sexual emanations (for Genet, fascism was entirely a sexual system in its conception and execution). His closest companion in the five months between his release from the Camp des Tourelles and the Liberation of Paris was the young Communist student and poet Jean Decarnin, with whom Genet had intermittently been engaged in the trading of stolen books since the early days of the Occupation.

As the Allied forces planned and undertook their invasion of France in the spring and early summer of 1944, Paris existed in suspension, anticipating the violent transmutation which the Germans' expulsion would bring about; already, the intricate arrangement of recrimination and self-aggrandizement that would animate and tear Paris in the Liberation's aftermath was starting to operate. The Germans' collaborators seeped away or reinvented themselves, apart from the militias that were inextricably meshed into the fascist forces. Genet spent those months in an acute poverty that was occasionally enlivened by momentary luxury after a successful theft, always occupying the most minute and cheapest rooms in the most disreputable or banal hotels. As well as pursuing his book-theft activities with Decarnin, along the Saint-Michel quayside and the Saint-Germain-des-Prés area's rare-book dealers,

Genet was developing his network of criminal contacts in Montmartre, among its population of drag queens, thugs, drug-dealers and pimps.

In later years, Genet would always declare that Jean Decarnin had been the most important lover in his life, along with the tightrope-walker Abdallah Bentaga, whom he met in the mid-1950s. Although Genet would write in his fiction of having sodom-ized Decarnin in his hotel room, Decarnin's friends and Genet's associates maintained that this was not the case and that Decarnin was a devoted political activist and heterosexual (and, in any case, Genet habitually preferred at this time to be a passive sexual recipient). The American army reached the Paris area in August and the city erupted into intensive fighting between young Resistance groups, of wide-ranging political convictions, and the remaining German forces with their French militia allies, many of whom had occupied rooftop vantage points for sniping. On 19 August 1944, six days before Paris's Liberation, Jean Decarnin's Trotskyite Resistance group were advancing for an attack on the Petite-Roquette prison (which then held captured Resistance fighters, although it had held Genet himself in 1926 during its existence as a children's prison); Decarnin was struck in the chest by a sniper's machine-gun fire and died on the same day at the Saint-Antoine hospital.

10

Jean Cocteau: Flaming Creature

During the same period towards the final stages of the German
Occupation when he was moving between prison incarcerations
and the criminal subterranea of Paris, Genet also encountered the
figure who would both launch the publication of his writings and
propel him into a literary socialization that was always a source of
ambivalent unease for Genet: Jean Cocteau. After their meeting,
Genet's life acquired another layer that existed in disjuncture with
the interchangeable strata of prison and criminality – and it was a
dimension that soon supplanted the others, bringing with it a
notoriety and celebrity that would make it impossible for Genet to
commit crimes in anonymity or to vanish entirely into the sensory
abyss of Montmartre. Cocteau, along with his associates in the
literary and artistic spheres of Paris, would even arrange for
Genet's crimes to be expunged by the French President (although
Genet was only provisionally pardoned, never amnestied – he still
retained the open-ended capacity to add to his accumulated convictions and risk life imprisonment). Genet's entire body changed
after his meeting with Cocteau: the corporeal zones of cruelty and
danger melted away and an elegantly dressed, less damaged Genet
appeared, for a moment at least.

Jean Cocteau's own extravagant celebrity in Paris had already
been established for thirty years, fuelled by his novels, theatre
works and films (especially *The Blood of a Poet*, which proved seminal
for all future experimental film-makers), by his opium addiction

and his all-consuming self-obsession. His attitude to the German Occupation was scrambled: attacked by the collaborationist media and once beaten-up by fascist thugs in the streets of Paris, he viewed the Occupation with equanimity and shared Hitler's admiration for the sculptor Arno Breker. He also had many young friends with pro-German sympathies, and one of them, Roland Laudenbach, took Genet to meet Cocteau after encountering him at the quayside bookstall where Genet worked with Decarnin. On 15 February 1943, Genet visited Cocteau at his apartment in the Palais Royal, where Cocteau lived with his lover, the actor Jean Marais, and Marais' own lover, Paul Morihien; he returned on the next day to read an extract from *Our Lady of the Flowers* to Cocteau. Although Cocteau was preoccupied with always discovering the most contemporary writing or art around him, and then promoting it, Genet's language startled him too much with its outrageous drag-queen narrative that veered wildly and fragmentarily in reverse, its explicit sex acts (Cocteau's homosexuality remained publicly oblique), and its overriding violence; initially, he was appalled. But after the first shock, he borrowed the manuscript of 'the Genet bomb', read it in one night and began to tell anyone that would listen that Genet was the most miraculous and astonishing writer of his time.

Cocteau instigated schemes by which *Our Lady of the Flowers* and Genet's other writings could be published clandestinely; he was convinced that Genet would have to remain a near-mystery, disseminated only by pre-warned connoisseurs of literary experimentation or pornography. But Genet, once he had overcome his resistance to being published at all, wanted his work to reach utterly unprepared readers, to exert its impact intact. He was soon engaged in quarrels with Paul Morihien, to whom Cocteau had delegated the task of serving as Genet's first publisher, and with Robert Denoël, whom Cocteau had persuaded to publish *Our Lady of the Flowers* covertly, with neither the name of the publisher nor the author on the cover (Denoël, who also published Louis-Ferdinand Céline and Antonin Artaud, was deeply involved in collaboration with the Germans and would be assassinated in the street at the war's end); independently of Cocteau, Genet also came into contact with the young publisher Marc Barbezat at the end of 1943 and beginning of 1944, while Genet was still imprisoned in the Santé and the Camp des Tourelles, and it was Barbezat's company, L'Arbalète, together with the much larger Gallimard, that became Genet's principal publishers in the decades to come. Although Cocteau introduced and lauded Genet to all of his associates in Paris, establishing his celebrity, their friendship was already becoming submerged by the time of the Liberation in recriminations over Cocteau's promotion of Genet, whose sudden notoriety both exhilarated and unnerved him. And it had also irresistibly placed him in a position of rivalry with Cocteau: after the war's end, Cocteau moved to a large house bought for him by Jean Marais in the village of Milly-la-Forêt, to the south of Paris, and began a series of films (notably, *Orphée* of 1950), whose success far exceeded that of Genet's own film projects of the same era, while Genet's novels had an ascendancy that surpassed Cocteau's own writings. To a large extent, Cocteau brought Genet into public existence, but that act of indulgence exploded in his face.

11

Funeral Rites

Genet's third novel, *Funeral Rites*, was written in the period
between the Liberation of Paris in August 1944 and the end of the
Second World War in the spring of the following year; it carries
all of the exultance, aberrance and massacre of that moment. The
gravity of Genet's language and the book's resistance towards its
reader (with its abrupt shifts in narrative voice and awry transfor-
mations of action and focus) conceal the provocations and out-
rages at its core, in which Genet lauds the Germans responsible
for atrocities on French civilians, visualizes Hitler in the act of
sodomizing the character of Jean Decarnin's brother, and pres-
ents Decarnin himself as a sacrifice to the desperate, treacherous
militiamen who machine-gunned Genet's companion during the
Liberation uprising. Genet conceived the novel as an elegy for
Decarnin, who appears – already dead at the book's opening –
both as Genet's lover and as the figure of death itself, whose tangible form generates Genet's exploration of the sensory juncture
between sex and death: in the novel's final scenes, the insolent
young militiaman Riton (whom Genet has seen in newsreel
footage of the Liberation and assigned as the killer of Jean
Decarnin), trapped on the rooftops of Paris and in imminent
danger of capture or death, performs his final acts of first having
sex with his German soldier companion and then capriciously
murdering him. In *Funeral Rites*, every act is propelled to its limit
until it reverses itself in violence or uproar. Having begun his

novel as an elegy to Decarnin, Genet transforms that book into a savage insult and betrayal of his friend; only in such extremity can memory survive.

Following Decarnin's funeral, Genet visits his friend's mother and meets Decarnin's brother, Paulo, and the mother's German lover, Erik, who has deserted from the now-defeated occupying forces and is in hiding. The two characters are propelled into Genet's hallucinations of death: Erik is dispatched to Berlin to become the lover of the city's executioner, then back to Paris as the soldier killed by Riton at the end of the book; Paolo suffers a still more grotesque and ludicrous transmutation in his sexual encounter with Hitler, who (still alive at the time of the writing of *Funeral Rites*) narrates his reflections on his own death:

> 'I was smiling. I was waiting for death. I knew it would come, violently, at the end of my adventure. Since, what did I finally desire? You do not rest after conquests: you enter, upright, into immortality. I've already been through every possible death: from death by poison, poured by a friend into my coffee, to being hanged by my own people, crucified by my best friends, not to mention a natural death surrounded by honours, music, flowers, speeches and statues, death in combat by a stabwound or bullets, but above all I dream of a vanishing that will astonish the world. I will leave to live calmly in another continent, observing the progression and damage wrought by the legend of my reappearance among my people. I have chosen every death. None could surprise me. I have often already died, and always in magnificence.'[11]

By inserting itself presciently and maliciously into the ongoing upheaval of Europe, as it collapsed into its final conflicts which would bring about the death both of Hitler and of millions more of its inhabitants, *Funeral Rites* already reverberates with the engulfing dynamics of atrocity, memory and oblivion which would also consume the postwar decades in Europe.

Funeral Rites, like all of Genet's work, is a book of death. In his distraught state at Decarnin's death, Genet imagines incorporating his friend's dead body into his own: stealing away with it from Decarnin's funeral ceremony, cutting it into pieces and then eating it in the form of flesh and ashes. His reinvention of Decarnin's death is projected through an angry assault and betrayal directed at that body, which intersects with the wounds inflicted upon the city and upon Europe itself; all of Genet's acts of death and mourning are vitally determined by his sexual obsessions, above all those directed towards the outcast figures of the teenaged militiamen high up on the city's rooftops, still virulently defiant and nonchalant as they await death. *Funeral Rites* forms a seduction, provocation and final repudiation of its reader, existing solely to incite Genet himself profoundly into life: 'Since I began writing this book, entirely devoted to the cult of a dead man in whose intimacy I live, I have experienced a kind of exaltation which, veiled by the alibi of the glory of Jean, is precipitating me towards a life that is more and more intense, more and more desperate: towards ever more audacity. I feel not only the strength to undertake more audacious burglaries, but also to fearlessly confront the most noble human institutions, in order to destroy them. I am drunk with life, with violence, with despair.'[12]

12

Genet in Liberated Paris

The Liberation of Paris in August 1944 created the conditions in which Genet could undertake an ascendancy into glory, although its raw components of celebrity, wealth and socialization proved unbearable assets for him. While his books were available only in covert or anonymous editions during the second half of the 1940s, their status as expensive, luxury items started to generate income for Genet; in particular, he now began to acquire rich patrons who bought the handwritten manuscripts of his novels (such as Jacques Guérin, the collector who owned Proust's bedroom and its entire contents, dismantled and dispatched to Guérin's mansion in Luzarches, to the north of Paris, where Genet began to make many visits). His sudden celebrity made him appear to have emerged from nowhere and enabled him to encounter the intellectual arbiters of post-Liberation Paris in the Saint-Germain-des-Prés cafés; although those cafés were crammed with new poets, all in hostile competition with one another, Genet's violently edged notoriety and the impact of his novels cleared an autonomous space for him. He had met Jean-Paul Sartre for the first time shortly before the Liberation, and their association of opposites grew over the late 1940s. Genet was able to change skins with alacrity, and his style of dress now marked the vast transformation of his life, from the near-fatal desperation of the Camp des Tourelles to the lavish literary celebrity of Saint-Germain-des-Prés, in the span of only a year or so. Genet had spent a large part of his life in the striped, harsh fabric of the penal uniform, in the soldier's uniform, or in the rags of his journeys across Europe; his new skin was that of handmade suits, monogrammed shirts and silk ties, all worn with a nonchalance that intimated they were a momentary apparition. The period after the Liberation was also that of Genet's most sustained explorations of Montmartre, accumulating contacts among the area's dense networks of prostitution, drug-dealing and sexual aberrance; Montmartre was a world unto itself at that moment, and Genet's motley collection of associates would be preserved on film at the end of the decade as the prisoners incarcerated in the cells of his film *Un Chant d'Amour*. Very few of the writers celebrated in post-Liberation Paris entered that world of pimps, criminals and drug-dealers (although Antonin Artaud, on his morphine-purchasing missions, was a regular visitor from 1946–8); its reverberations gradually entered Genet's style of dress, so that by the end of the 1940s it had changed again, into the still-dandified zipped jackets and jerseys which he would wear to the end of his life, as a compound of uniform and oblivious elegance.

Paris itself underwent vast transmutation on its surface skin in the period following the Liberation, while remaining profoundly invariable at its core (even the turmoil of demonstrations in which Genet would participate twenty years later, in May 1968, failed to dislodge that repressive stasis). The skeletal figures returning from the concentration camps, and housed in a grand hotel on the boulevard Raspail, formed both a jarring revelation of Europe's calamities for the compromised inhabitants of undestroyed Paris, and also a livid though silent reproach – the police and citizens of Paris had been among the most assiduous in Europe in assisting or colluding with the Germans in their deportations to concentration camps of Jewish inhabitants, particularly in the 'Vél d'Hiv' round-ups of 1942. The recriminations over collaboration with the Germans (blurred and exacerbated by the extent to which Paris's citizens attempted wholesale to reinvent their actions of the four years of

German Occupation) penetrated every level of the city's life, before dispersing into uneasy silence with the Gaullist projection of France as having been mystically, wholly resistant during the war. To a large extent, in that city of lies, it was the greatest fabricator of all, Genet, who was telling the truth. The imperative need to confront the lacerated or extinguished human form unleashed a vast experimentation with corporeal matter in art at that moment of the Liberation and through to the end of the 1940s, in the painting and sculpture of figures such as Henri Michaux, Jean Fautrier and, above all, Alberto Giacometti, who would work intimately with Genet in the following decade. The desire to bring into existence reactivated images of the human body, from an irreparably damaged material, was always pinioned between the presences of death and sex; both the visual art of postwar Paris and Genet's own language hold the gestures of that excavation.

13

Querelle of Brest

The city of Brest is a uniquely peripheral site for Genet: at the far edge of France, and of Europe, it is engulfed by the presence of the ocean which disgorges a perpetual stream of murderous, sexually alert sailors into its fog-hidden alleyways. Brest forms the location for Genet's fourth novel, *Querelle of Brest*, begun in 1945. Although Brest had been largely destroyed during wartime bombing, it bears no trace of its recent calamity in Genet's novel, in which the city's topography exists solely to channel its characters from one act of obsession to another. *Querelle of Brest* is the only one of Genet's novels to be projected as a third-person narrative with invented characters: every element of its narrative becomes doubled as Genet conjures two feuding brothers, two competing but loving murderers, and dually shattered identities for all of the characters. But even in his creation of his most sealed narrative world, Genet himself still intermittently bursts forward, to emphasize how he propels his characters into acts of murder and his city into sensory intensification in order to receive, by return, a sexual or vertiginous charge of his own; he also adds a scattering of contemporary elements into the novel's volatile mix, evoking an account of the commandant of the Drancy transit camp (the complex of concrete-block tenements, close to Paris, where its condemned inhabitants were corralled prior to dispatch to the German concentration camps). At the heart of Genet's Brest are the two forms of an infamous brothel, La Feria, and of a now-abandoned but imposing prison:

'The double coat-of-arms of France and of Brittany forms the main decoration of the majestic pediment of the Brest prison, where the architectural designs represent naval seafaring. Placed side by side, the two oval coats-of-arms are not flat but bulging, swollen. They possess the importance of a sphere whose sculptor has forgotten to polish it, but whose totality imparts to these fragments its absolute power.'[13]

Even in its state of often-raw corporeal interrogation, Genet's novel transmits an intact aura of glory to its acts of murder and sodomy.

Immediately upon the arrival of his ship in Brest, the sailor Querelle murders his partner in an opium-smuggling operation, slitting his throat on the deserted ramparts above the port. For the entirety of the novel, Querelle then manoeuvres the other characters into arrangements that will allow his crime to be screened from detection. These manoeuvres extend from nonchalantly offering himself up to be sodomized by the brothel's owner, Nono, and by its resident police inspector, Mario, to conceiving of an intricate plan enabling him to allocate his own crime to the responsibility of another murderer, Gil, who is hiding in the derelict prison building. Only by forming an intimate attachment to Gil is Querelle able to countenance the act of betrayal which will transfer the power of his crime with all of its prestige and glory intact. And Genet calls on his reader to witness or participate in that transmutation exacted by language, which can also elevate itself from the lowliest popular literature, to acquire the status of art:

'Only the most execrable literature, it seems to me, could write of a painting representing the infant Jesus: "In his gaze and smile, the sadness and despair of the crucifixion can already be discerned". However, in order to reach the truth of the relationship between Gil and Querelle, the reader must allow me to make use of the same appalling literary platitudes which I condemn, in order to enable me to write that Gil suddenly experienced a premonition of his betrayal by Querelle and of his own sacrifice. This mark of literary banality not only has the use of locating more rapidly and effectively the roles of the two heroes; there remains something else, which I will discover along with the reader.'[14]

Genet arranges a schematic template for the exploration of death and treachery in his novel, and seductively lures the reader into that precarious framework; only its urban components – the evanescing, fog-shrouded apparitions of Brest – are solidly constructed. Querelle definitively betrays Gil, denouncing him to the police, but every other element of the novel is left gapingly open for the reader.

Towards the end of the novel, space disintegrates and time escalates: Genet declares that he has now become exasperated with his own characters, whose narrative momentum has sedimented into stasis. The process of narration itself implodes, and Genet seeks refuge in the fragments of journal entries kept by Querelle's commanding officer, Lieutenant Seblon, as he condenses his infatuation with the sailor into the delineation of corporeal gestures performed by Querelle on his ship, and into notated accounts of his own journeys through the vanishing city, searching for traces of Querelle. Only those pure or aberrant sensations subsist as Genet's novel intentionally runs aground. But the very openness of *Querelle of Brest* – half-botched, suddenly abandoned, and veering into wild sensory disarray – itself proved a provocatively irresistible incitation for its readers, most notably in the form of Rainer Werner Fassbinder's 1982 film of the book, which itself opens out its images for every form of penetration and spectatorial participation.

14

Genet's Hotel Rooms

Genet moved restlessly in the late 1940s, from hotel to hotel and between Paris and the south coast of France, especially Cannes. In the intervals between his prison stays of the early 1940s, he had always inhabited the most abject or negligently run hotels (those from which he could make rapid escapes, without paying his bill and often taking the sheets from his bed along with him, rolled around his waist); now, with the money from his books and manuscript sales, he began to stay at more luxurious hotels, notably the Terrass hotel above the Montmartre cemetery (where he had occasionally stayed even during the most wretched of his earlier periods in Paris – the views from the top floor windows of the Terrass correspond to those of Divine's attic room in *Our Lady of the Flowers*). It was in the lobby of the Terrass that Genet was detained by the police for the final time in France, to be questioned over the outstanding fine that remained from his multiple convictions of the beginning of the 1940s. But Genet's inhabitation of luxury was short-lived; soon, he would return to the regime of lowly or undistinguished Paris hotels (such as the one in which his life would end, forty years later) that provided him with anonymity and the potential for sudden exits. Genet was living nowhere; in bed, all night, smoking endless cigarettes, he wrote his novels, usually in cheap exercise books or on scraps of paper which he then assembled together, detaching and reconstructing the mass of paper until the fragments of acts and sequences of narration had been

Genet in Paris, 1947. Photo by Brassaï.

adhered into the form he desired. He would also take the contents of half-finished or abandoned novels and insert them into his work in progress; both *Miracle of the Rose* and *Funeral Rites* incorporated elements from disparate projects, sometimes with a jarring or incongruous impact on the novel into which they became embedded (Genet would write new, hallucinatory sequences to mesh the components together). His hotel rooms became swamped in paper; since Genet often wrote several successive versions of the same novel, in intensive bursts of work, the manuscripts became scrambled, lost and torn. He also destroyed manuscripts in his hotel rooms, particularly if a friend or lover to whom he read or lent the manuscript responded with any degree of criticism; although most of his works survived that destruction through their existence in multiple variants, Genet would occasionally burn or shred the sole manuscript of his works (as happened with an early play, *Heliogabalus*, which Cocteau's lover Jean Marais had slighted). Whenever Genet changed hotels, all of the debris of notebooks and papers would have to be bundled up and taken with him.

Genet came to the end both of his crimes and his novels at the close of the 1940s. Although he continued to perform occasional burglaries (usually in collaboration with younger friends) after his release from the Camp des Tourelles in 1944, Genet was never again arrested. Indulged by the police chiefs of Paris, such as Maurice Toesca (who, especially after the Occupation years, were well-aware of the ephemeral boundary between institutional brutality or criminality and individual crime), Genet was protected both by his celebrity and the devoted professionalism of his new accomplices. As he exhausted his crimes, and found himself pardoned by the French President at Cocteau's and Sartre's instigation, Genet also reached the last use of the raw material derived from his own past life in his final novel, *The Thief's Journal*, in which he both scoured his journeys of the mid-1930s for memory traces of abjection and also brought his work crashing into the immediacy of the present moment. That exhaustion would eventually lead Genet to expel or exile himself from his inhabitation of Paris hotel rooms, with his incessant journeys of the following decade through Greece, Italy and other countries; but it was an abandonment conducted from one void to another, between instantly replicable and replaceable spaces cohered only by sex acts and by the momentary presences of Genet's accumulated, shredded manuscripts.

Jean Genet, by the painter and actor Jean Marais (1947, oil on canvas).

15

The Thief's Journal

The Thief's Journal is a book of deep solitude, in which Genet
recounts his movements across Europe on foot in the 1930s;
although he encounters criminals and forms sexual relationships
with them in every city he traverses, Genet constructs for himself
an isolation cell around his body as he travels, since only that profound separation from every other human being can enable him to
compound the aura of abject glory through which he survives.
All time and space is subjugated to the exigencies of that journey
into the self, with the desiccated landscapes of Andalusia and the
marine cityscapes of Antwerp enveloping but never penetrating
that journey. In his final novel, begun in 1946 and published
in 1948, Genet resuscitates his travels of the mid-1930s into a
grandiose incursion into the nature of death and solitude; as his
clothes rot to rags on the coasts of Spain and his hold on the world
deteriorates, Genet projects himself as an ever more unique and
radiant figure, whose exclusion from every habitual means of life
serves only to render him incandescent with glory. Although
Genet's actual travels across Europe extended for no more than a
year, they become endlessly diffused in *The Thief's Journal* (which
intimates that the journey lasted almost throughout the 1930s):
time itself is conjured away and vanishes. Only in the sexual acts
Genet narrates does duration resurge – time is then aggressively
concertinaed into brutality and ecstasy. In his accounts of his relationships with his criminal lovers, Armand and Stilitano (whom

Genet first encounters in the dirt-encrusted alleyways of Barcelona's Barri Xinès district and meets again in Antwerp), Genet above all emphasizes their oblivion towards him; their engagement is solely located within the labyrinthine demands of crime, and their violent indifference to Genet (articulated both by sexual acts and argot-inflected reproaches) consolidates his solitude. Only when he inadvertently catches glimpses of gestures of love, in the wretched sites he moves between, does Genet's solitude shatter for a moment:

'On the coasts of the Atlantic and those of the Mediterranean, I passed through ports of fishermen whose elegant poverty wounded my own. Without them seeing me, I brushed against men and women standing in patches of shade, boys playing in the square. Then, the love which these human beings seemed to hold for one another tore me. As I passed, two young men exchanged a greeting, a smile, and I was thrown outwards to the most extreme corners of the world.'[15]

Genet's sudden pain is exacerbated by his impression that the words exchanged by the young men contain an arrangement for their sexual encounter that same night; his exclusion from that act both lacerates him and reinforces his magisterial solitude.

In every place he traverses, Genet steals: he cracks open the offerings-box in churches, offers himself for prostitution to older homosexuals and then robs them, and plans burglaries or drugs robberies with his associates. As long as he experiences his acts as existing in tension with the world surrounding him, and subject to the punitive outrage of that world, Genet is able to hold his projected glory of criminality intact. But when, on his travels, he reaches Berlin, his deviance and uniqueness are abruptly over-turned and cancelled-out:

'To reach Antwerp, I crossed Hitler's Germany, where I stayed for several months. I walked from Breslau to Berlin. I wanted to steal. A strange force prevented me. Germany was terrifying the entirety of Europe; especially in my eyes, it had become the symbol of cruelty. It was already beyond the law. Even on the Unter den Linden, I had the feeling that I was walking within a camp organized by bandits. I believed that the brain of the most conscientious, bourgeois Berliner hid treasures of duplicity, hatred, malice, cruelty, covetousness. I was moved by my freedom within a population that was entirely subjugated. I certainly could have stolen there, just as elsewhere; but I experienced a kind of torment, since that which directed that city's activity and resulted from it – this particular moral attitude established as a civic virtue – was known by an entire nation and directed against other nations. This is a population of thieves, I told myself. If I steal here, I will accomplish no special action which could allow me to better realize myself. I would be obeying the habitual system. I would not destroy it. I would commit no evil, disturb nothing. Scandal would be impossible, theft would be void . . . In Berlin, I decided to live by prostitution. I enjoyed it for a few days, then it bored me.'[16]

Genet's time in Berlin demonstrates to him that the contrariness and aberration which underpin his life are utterly dependent on the society which encompasses him; in cities such as Antwerp and Barcelona, his opposition to that urban society and its detestation of him ensure he will never be incorporated by the environment which surrounds him, and from whose matter he can generate his acts of crime. Hitler's Germany has the same impact of dissolution on Genet as its extension in Paris during the Occupation, particularly in the form of the French militia, composed of young thugs and criminals, which terrorized the city on behalf of the Germans. As Genet narrates in *Funeral Rites*, the furious loathing of the population of Paris towards that once-powerful, now-desperate force, at the moment of the Liberation, could only make Genet himself empathize with that endangered police of thieves.

The Thief's Journal is a novel about hotel rooms (the insect-ridden and filthy hotel rooms of Barcelona and the dank, equally minuscule hotel rooms of Antwerp), written in hotel rooms. Towards the end of the novel, the presence of Genet's current hotel room in Paris becomes predominant, just as Genet's lovers of his 1930s journeys, Armand and Stilitano, are supplanted by his current lovers, Lucien and Java. In one of the final sequences of the novel, the now-wealthy Genet is walking with Java through the Saint-Ouen fleamarket on the northern periphery of Paris; they encounter Guy, Genet's former lover from the Santé prison and the model for the character Bulkaen in *Miracle of the Rose*. Guy is now poverty stricken and filthy, attempting to sell the sheets he has just stolen from a hotel. He is as wretched as Genet during his journey of ultimate abjection through Andalusia, the account of which forms the first part of *The Thief's Journal*. After a momentary exchange with his humiliated friend, Genet recoils. All of his five novels had now become entangled in his own body and in its history of sex and criminality. With *The Thief's Journal* (which Genet announces as being his last novel, while contrarily promising a sequel), his work finally exhausts that body and its history, and strikes the immediacy of the present moment.

16

Lucien, Java, Decimo

After completing *The Thief's Journal* – the last of five intensive and
innovative novels undertaken in less than five years – Genet never
again wrote fiction; for the next seven or eight years, until the
mid-1950s, he wrote almost nothing at all. His celebrity in France
accumulated as his creative activity declined. During those years,
Genet became preoccupied with film projects, to some degree in
ambivalent reaction to Cocteau's own cinema, which had successfully taken its author into a new arena of work. But they were also
years in which Genet was deeply involved with his three successive
lovers of the period: Lucien Sénémaud, André Babkine and Decimo
Cristiani. His relationships expanded to full-time occupations at
times, since Genet conceived of his responsibility to his lovers as
involving the reinvention of their lives, interspersed with moments
of furious repudiation. Most of Genet's lovers of this period were
young heterosexual men with backgrounds in criminality, fascism
or prostitution; Genet travelled with them on his extensive journeys of the period, introduced them to his friends in Paris, and
envisaged putting them into his film projects. None of them had
any interest in Genet's writings: they responded to his capricious
desperation for them, to his wealth, and to the attraction of his
glamorous notoriety.

Lucien Sénémaud was eighteen and a sulky hoodlum when
Genet met him in Cannes in 1945. Although he committed thefts
while living and travelling with Genet, Lucien already had a child

and Genet was aware that he wanted to settle into a family life – a prospect that both horrified Genet and incited his sense of protective responsibility. During their years together, Genet transformed his relationship with Lucien into the diverse media he was working in: into fiction, in *The Thief's Journal* (where Lucien, almost always indifferent, is tortured, adored and vilified); into poetry, in Genet's poem of 1946, *The Fisherman of Suquet* (the Suquet is a district of Cannes); and into cinema, with Lucien's role as a prisoner in Genet's 1950 film *Un Chant d'Amour*. Genet decided to build a house for Lucien, and used money from his manuscript sales to construct a large villa in Le Cannet, a hillside suburb of Cannes; a room was reserved in the house for Genet, though he would rarely use it. Genet also decided that Lucien should marry an older woman named Ginette who already had two children by another man. Finally, he set Lucien up as a garage proprietor; in the 1990s, Lucien was still active as the oil-sodden, grizzled owner of a car-repair shed bearing the sign 'Garage Saint-Genet'.

Whereas Lucien resembled Genet as a young man, André Babkine was a more fiercely attractive and heavily built man, when Genet met him in 1947 (at the time when he was constructing a socialized life for Lucien). They also met in Cannes, where the twenty-two-year-old Babkine was working on a yacht, the 'Java', whose name Genet gave to his new lover. In a talk he gave on Genet in Italy in 1989, Java remembered that he was about to enlist for service in the Indo-China colonial war (he had fought for the Germans during the Second World War) at the time when he was introduced to Genet, 'a little man with a boxer's nose'.[17] Java abandoned his army plans to live and travel with Genet for over five years; as with Lucien Sénémaud, he was incorporated into *The Thief's Journal* (which Genet was completing at the time of their meeting). Java continued relationships with women during his years with Genet, who always wanted to hear about Java's sexual activities; Genet and Java had sex only intermittently, while Genet favoured teenage prostitutes. Java had no interest in Genet's novels: 'I'm not literary. I understand nothing of his writings.' But Genet was vital to him: 'He made me live.'[18] As with Lucien, Genet set Java up in business at the end of their relationship (with a dry-cleaning shop in the south of France), but Java took independent action, to Genet's disapproval, in choosing his own wife. Java died in the mid-1990s.

Genet's relationship with Decimo Cristiani had an exactly inverse impact on him to those sustaining, involving relationships with Lucien and Java, the power dynamics of which were almost always inflected in Genet's favour. Decimo, a young homosexual prostitute from Rome whom Genet met in 1952, transmitted a cruelty and calamity into Genet's life which would almost always also be present in his future relationships. Although Genet planned to give Decimo a role in his current film project, *The Penal Colony*, the oblivious Decimo abruptly rejected Genet, who experienced that cold rejection as a silencing, irreparable shattering.

17

Nico Papatakis and Genet

Through the nightclub owner Nico Papatakis, Genet was able to begin to realize his film projects in 1950; though he was to formulate many film projects from then until his death, that first film, *Un Chant d'Amour*, was also Genet's last. He had encountered Nico Papatakis in Saint-Germain-des-Prés in 1943; Papatakis was then in his mid-twenties, and would stay put in Saint-Germain-des-Prés for the rest of his life. He had been born in 1918 in Ethiopia, of Greek and Ethiopian parentage, and arrived in Paris to train as an actor shortly before the Second World War. A strikingly beautiful man even in his eighties, Papatakis had an immediate impact on Paris, where he would embody the city's creative and intellectual frenzy of the late 1940s and early 1950s, with its core in the cafés and clubs around Saint-Germain-des-Prés. But at the time of their first meeting, Papatakis and Genet were both desperately poor; they worked in collaboration on burglaries, but their friendship was heated – on one occasion, when Genet received money from his writing, he taunted Papatakis in the street with the mass of bank notes, then called the police when Papatakis, unbearably incited, tried to snatch the money away.

By the end of the 1940s, Papatakis was himself wealthy from the profits of his nightclub, La Rose Rouge, which had opened in 1946 in the rue de Rennes and rapidly became the focal point of all the young artists, philosophers and writers in Saint-Germain-des-Prés. When Genet told Papatakis of his ambition to make a film,

A set built above La Rose Rouge nightclub for Genet's 1950 film *Un Chant d'Amour*.

Papatakis had the money and the space to indulge Genet: the subterranean nightclub was located beneath a large restaurant room which Papatakis left empty, and the sets for Genet's film – a network of dirt-encrusted prison cells – were constructed in that space. Although Papatakis put up the money for the film and would own it, Genet himself chose his actors: Lucien Sénémaud in a main part and Java in a subordinate role (only his arm is visible as he swings roses on a string from one cell window to another), together with a motley collection of pimps and thugs from Genet's circle of Montmartre associates; none of the actors were professionals. Part of the film was also shot in the rocky woodlands around Milly-la-Forêt, to the south of Paris, where Cocteau had recently acquired a house; Cocteau attended the outdoor shooting, though he did not participate in the direction of the film, which Genet undertook alone, instructing the professional technicians whom Papatakis had hired. Several shots were filmed clandestinely

of the walls of the Santé prison in Paris. After the film was completed in June 1950, Papatakis set about selling individual film prints to
collectors such as Jacques Guérin; in the context of that moment in
cinema history, Genet's film was pornography, its public screening
illegal worldwide (for Papatakis, France in particular was and
remains the most repressive and culturally stultified country in the
world). Genet rapidly moved on to his subsequent film projects,
and left Papatakis with the work of recouping the costs of the film.

Whereas all of Genet's future film projects would go unrealized,
collapsing one after the other in acrimony or creative despair,
Papatakis himself would go on to make a handful of extraordinary
films (including two films obliquely derived from Genet's work:
Les Abysses and *The Tightrope-Walkers*); Papatakis also left Saint-
Germain-des-Prés temporarily for New York, where he worked as a
film producer with the director John Cassavetes and promoted the
careers of his many female lovers, notably the singer with Andy
Warhol's Velvet Underground group, Nico (who took Papatakis's
first name as her own). Papatakis lived a life of provocation, riling
censorship bodies with his films and attempting to explore volatile
subject-matters – revolution, sexual torture and subjugation –
which resonated with Genet's own obsessions. Papatakis was often
impoverished, and his final dispute with Genet in the mid-1970s,
like his first, was over money; Papatakis slyly arranged to be given
a producer's film prize for *Un Chant d'Amour*, presenting it as
though it were Genet's most recent work. Genet had now come
to dislike his decades-old film, and he furiously demanded that
Papatakis give his prize money back, ending their friendship.
Despite his own film works, Papatakis in old age remained embit-
teredly swamped by the overriding presence of Genet on his life.

18

Un Chant d'Amour

The figures in Genet's film *Un Chant d'Amour* are those of prisoners
in crepuscular, excrementally inscribed cells whose sole purpose
is to serve as spatial concentrations for the sexual obsessions and
intricate power rapports of those confined figures. No gestures or
traces of punishment subsist in the film; even when a guard beats a
prisoner and inserts his pistol into the prisoner's mouth, it forms
an ecstatic sexual act that meshes with the prisoners' other gestures
of sexual transmission or desperation: the blowing of cigarette
smoke from eager mouth to mouth via a straw through a hole
which has miraculously appeared in the wall between two cells, or
the battering with a fist and erect penis by one prisoner to attract
the attention of the prisoner in the adjacent cell. Even the most
brutal acts of violence in the film are those of seduction. The guard
witnesses a succession of figures in provocative or insolent poses of
sexual self-immersal as he passes from spyhole to spyhole along the
prison corridor; every isolated figure constitutes a sensory world in
himself that cancels out any emanation of social retribution from
the prison. But the film's acts are still locked in repetition; even
when the film's North African prisoner (played by one of Genet's
Montmartre associates) succeeds in beguiling and penetrating the
younger, arrogant prisoner (played by Lucien Sénémaud) through
the medium of smoke, he must immediately begin again, pounding
his fist in exasperation as he tries to formulate a new medium of
seduction. Every act in the film is consumed and incorporated

Genet's lover Lucien Sénémaud in *Un Chant d'Amour*.

within that endless oscillation between sexual elation and incapacitation.

The walls of the prison cells that Papatakis's designers had constructed in the nightclub space form porous, unstable screens (seen to rock at one point in the film), and they can also instantaneously evanesce: as the North African prisoner is being beaten by the guard, the space of the film abruptly transmutates in his imagination or memory to that of a forest landscape, where he pursues the younger prisoner and finally ensnares him; while the guard is violating the prisoner with his pistol, he simultaneously visualizes other sexual spaces and corporeal constellations, as naked male bodies move over one another in gestures of anal penetration or fellatio, set against total darkness. Flesh, as in Genet's novels, is a fragile, transforming matter whose transmission is rendered through the medium of flowers: the flower seized out of the mouth of one figure by another in the guard's imagination, or the roses swung from one hand to another, from one cell window to another, against the exterior wall of the prison. That wall is the only surface not overwritten by Genet's images; at the end of the film, the guard walks away against the massive, unbreachable wall of the Santé prison. But the final image of the film, in which the sparse details of the film's existence (such as its date) are graffitied against a cell or prison wall, reinstates that desire to indelibly engrave the gestures of sex and resistance, and to simultaneously obliterate the gestures of power and punishment.

The survival of *Un Chant d'Amour*, in the decades after its making, itself formed the opposition of a fragile medium (the celluloid of its film prints, battered by multiple projections) to an engulfing social and judicial environment. The film was often censored, its screenings violently broken-up and terminated by the police, especially in the United States. Existing only in the medium of images (no script or text on the film by Genet has ever been found, and he gave it no soundtrack), the film disappeared from sight for years at a time, reappearing in ever-diminished forms as the celluloid faded and collectors snipped frames of erect penises or forcibly opened mouths from its film-reel. Genet himself played no part in the survival of his film after he had brought it into existence; dubious about its worth, or preoccupied with new film projects, he neglected *Un Chant d'Amour*, engaging with it again in the mid-1970s only to repudiate it in his dispute with Papatakis. The status of the film as an intricately disintegrating, vilified or adored object then abruptly changed in 2003, with the transferral of Papatakis's original negative of the film into a digital document and its release as a DVD: its duration of twenty-five minutes now contracted or expanded into the infinitely volatile medium of its spectator's perception and concentration, while its space mutated into the form of any digital image-screen. From its original existence as a covert experiment in pornography (the sale of each film-print to its wealthy collectors being presented as that of a unique, irreplaceable

A scene from *Un Chant d'Amour*.

object), to its tenuous cinematic projections in subsequent decades as a legally threatened, materially torn object, *Un Chant d'Amour* in its DVD medium now returned to the unique, original form of its conception, though that form became as exposed to being capriciously reformulated and overridden by its spectator as that of the prison walls over and against which Genet had inscribed his images in 1950.

19

The Penal Colony

Genet planned other film projects to follow on from *Un Chant d'Amour*. That film formed a secret fragment, impossible to project in the cinemas of Paris and distributed covertly to one-man audiences of wealthy collectors; however, the cinema Genet wanted to make was vaster in scale, able to realize entire cities of incarceration and corporeal obsession, for audiences that needed to be both assaulted by the provocations of Genet's images and simultaneously made conscious of that assault and its origin. Two years after his first film, Genet was preparing to make another, *The Penal Colony*, which he planned to direct in a studio in Rome, with his lover Decimo Cristiani in the main role of the convict Forlano, who arrives at the penal colony with the glory of his crimes in France intact, but has to be allocated another crime (the murder of a guard) in his new world of the colony, in order to attain the supreme glory of an execution by guillotine. The penal colonies of France, such as those in French Guiana, including Devil's Island, situated on the other side of the world in profoundly inhospitable landscapes, had been officially abolished in 1938, fourteen years before Genet wrote his filmscript; the convicts had gradually been released or transferred to prisons in France in the intervening years, and Genet's planned film would articulate his hallucinated nostalgia for a punitive system that had now irreparably vanished, while allowing him to reconfigure that system to meet his own sexual and creative exigencies.

Genet's penal colony is distinct from the actual colonies of France, which were surrounded by oceans or impenetrable tropical forests; Genet situates his own colony in a desert of extreme heat and sparseness:

'The penal colony is fixed in the middle of a desert: a desert of stones rather than sand: an immense plain, burned by the sun. No plants grow. The camera must photograph these stones with precision, showing their glittering surfaces which contain mica. The penal colony needs to be shown as existing at the centre of an aridity that is perfect, mineral and crystallized . . . Time there is always the same. It never rains. Unless I decide to mention them, there are never storms. And no animals, except for flies: at certain moments, they form thick, excessive black clouds.'[19]

In his notes accompanying the filmscript, Genet emphasizes that the prisoners' gestures too are curtailed to the point of an immediate, brutal expressivity, occasionally supplemented by dense, expectorated cries and phrases in argot. Everything has been cut to the bone in the penal colony, so that the narrative of Forlano's arrival, interaction with the other prisoners and execution is rendered with excoriating brevity, between Genet's evocations of the prisoners' infinitely repeated rituals, walking in disciplined circles around the punishment yard. Even the murder of the prison guard (executed on Forlano's behalf by another prisoner, Rocky) is immediate, undertaken in one gesture: like the guard in *Un Chant d'Amour*, the penal colony guard is peering through the cells' spyholes at the prisoners; a long needle thrust through a spyhole from the other side pierces his eye and kills him instantly. Such a gesture of ocular violation has its implications too for Genet's potential spectators, who are seduced into the colony's world of naked prisoners (who must discard their uniforms before entering their cells), then lacerated by its aura of burning heat and abrupt acts of violence. The only sumptuous moment in Genet's filmscript, cancelling that skeletal aridity of space, language and corporeal gesture, takes the form of the lavish outpouring of Forlano's blood after he has been decapitated:

> 'Everyone – apart from the chaplain, who is praying – watches in fascination as the convict picks up Forlano's head by the ears. He passes it to Ferrand, who gazes fixedly at it before enveloping it in a white cloth which rapidly turns scarlet. The second assistant carries the decapitated body to a coffin whose length is that of a body without a head. The blood flows, red on the white sand of the courtyard. The flies are there, black and compact . . . So, photograph the floods of blood, photograph the thickness, the weight and the colour of the blood. Photograph, in close-up, the fingers of the assistant carrying the head by the ears: fingers covered in blood.'[20]

The Penal Colony visualizes a filmic world with excruciating exactitude and anticipation; it would prove to be the last of Genet's sustained works on spaces of incarceration and their dynamics of sexual tension and disintegrating grandeur. Although Genet was at the height of his notoriety at the moment when he wrote the filmscript, he would never direct it. It rapidly became tainted in Genet's eyes through Decimo Cristiani's rejection of him (Decimo showed a supreme insolence and indifference to Genet's plans to cast him in the film, exactly mirroring the blasé contempt of the film's own characters); he would destroy the final manuscript of the filmscript a decade or so later, in his despair over the suicide of his lover of that time, Abdallah Bentaga, although it survived in the form of another manuscript. While *Un Chant d'Amour* exists only in the medium of images, without a filmscript or soundtrack, *The Penal Colony* has an inverse presence: lacking the images which Genet had envisaged, its medium is that of a savagely reduced language, throbbing with insect noise and its expelled human cries.

20

Genet's Film Projects

Genet confronted the cinema at the moment when he had exhausted his fiction, with the sequence of novels that ended with *The Thief's Journal*. But even the raw material of his novels had possessed the capacity to project itself into the form of films at the time when he had begun writing those novels. At his first meeting with Genet in October 1942, François Sentein (who would help Genet with the publication of *Our Lady of the Flowers*, which Genet was working on at that time) noted in his journal that Genet had evoked for him 'a film which would depict a prison colony for children, in the shadow of a vast prison for adults: a presence which the children dream about, which raises them up and captivates them'.[21] Genet was speaking about the preoccupations – already visualized, in images – that would collect into his subsequent novel, *Miracle of the Rose*. Genet's novels, with their intricate processes of flashbacks and flashforwards, their close-ups and dense superimpositions, were conceived filmically, in the isolation of Genet's prison cells or at liberty in Paris, before their transmutation into language. It was only through the intermediation of an entrepreneur such as Papatakis (and later, of professional film producers such as Claude Nedjar) that Genet could have access to the funds and technological media essential for his film projects; by contrast, all his novels required were a pen and any surface (even the roughest, most resistant surfaces, such as those of prison sacks) to write upon, in any physical circumstances. All of Genet's novels formed filmic projects that were aberrantly diverted into another

Genet with a film camera, Luzarches, 1950.

medium, and gained in contrary tension from that movement; as novels, Genet's obsessions emerged fully formed and with rapidity (even in the crammed cells of the Camp des Tourelles, in danger of deportation, Genet kept writing at high speed), while as film projects, after 1950, they relentlessly collapsed and immobilized themselves, often at Genet's own instigation.

Genet worked endlessly on film projects from *The Penal Colony* in 1952 to a large-scale documentary film about Mettray which he abandoned in 1982, *The Language of the Wall*, which was intended to weld factual accounts of Mettray's origins to hallucinatory sequences in which the long-dead founders of the colony and its imprisoned children, often killed by their solitary incarceration in punishment cells, would insurge as apparitions into the filmic space. In the intervening thirty years, Genet wrote thousands of pages of film notes, treatments and scripts, spending entire years developing projects before capriciously sweeping them into abandonment at the moment when they became capable of realization. They were decades in which Genet often preferred to articulate his preoccupations through silence or fragments rather than in completed works. He sometimes worked with directors or scenarists on projects to make films from his novels, though his participation invariably took the form of slyly overturning the project or of taking as much money as he could from his collaborators before abruptly vanishing (the only one of Genet's novels to be successfully filmed, *Querelle of Brest*, was transformed back into images without Genet's participation). In the 1970s, Genet worked for a period of two years on writing an original script for a project entitled *The Fall of Night*, on the journey of a young Moroccan through a grotesque and hostile cityscape of Paris before his decision to return to his home village; Genet spent many nights scouring the streets of Paris with his collaborators to find suitable shooting locations, and the film was cast and fully financed. Then, Genet abandoned it (to the fury of his collaborators), the arbitrariness of his withdrawal sustaining his habitual involvement with and then abrupt renunciation of his film projects. Genet's unease encompassed both the technological media of cinema, whose interventions would layer themselves over his own preoccupations, and also the fixed duration and location of a film-shoot's schedule, which would overrule the flux of time and space Genet inhabited.

Cinema was a perpetual preoccupation for Genet from his experience of the open-air film screenings of his childhood in Alligny, until his death. The only images that subsist from that long engagement are those of his one short film, *Un Chant d'Amour*, within a vast terrain of abandoned or destroyed scripts and projects. Integral to Genet's obsession with film after 1950 was his refusal of it, exacerbated in turn, with *The Penal Colony*, by Decimo Cristiani's refusal of Genet himself. Genet's film images were often a means to cohere and visualize male anatomies, in crisis or ecstasy, for his own sexual incitation and gratification; but as Genet's life began to disintegrate into silence, fractured words and blank images after 1950, the medium of cinema – in many ways, the perfect one for the realization of Genet's imageries – also fell apart and cancelled itself out in his work.

Genet in Paris, 1951.

21

The Cock and the Anus

In the gap of silence between Genet's film *Un Chant d'Amour* of
1950 and the resurgence of his work in the mid-1950s, the explicit
charge of obscenity and pornography largely disappeared from his
work; up until that point, Genet had always saturated his narra-
tives with evocations of enormous, omniscient penises whose
corporeal eminence accords them the status of being characters in
their own right in his novels; similarly, in Genet's densely evoked
sex scenes (such as that, in *Our Lady of the Flowers*, in which Seck
Gorgui gleefully sodomizes Our Lady of the Flowers who is simultaneously fellated by Divine), the presence of the anus – as a trans-
parent medium, a fragile screen, or an eye to be violently pierced –
is highlighted as magisterial in its glory and is determining. In the
context of the 1940s, Genet's novels had an impact of astonishment
in France; no other writer of Genet's stature had propelled himself
headlong into an area viewed as obscene or extreme, with his
exhaustive descriptions of homosexual sex acts between white and
black men, between Nazi soldiers and French militiamen, and
between the living and the dead. In *Funeral Rites*, the sequence in
which Hitler himself narrates his own intensive sexual encounter
with a young Frenchman, appalled and awed its readers. But above
all, it was the figure of the drag queen Divine, desperately obsessed
by the penises of her criminal lovers, that possessed the greatest
inspiration in the worldwide sexual impact of Genet's novels in the
1960s, serving as the driving force behind the New York Stonewall

riots of 1969 (the seminal act of gay liberation in the USA) and behind the explosive mix of sexual and revolutionary experimentation in Tokyo's Shinjuku district during the same period. The impetus of Genet's sex acts transformed imageries of sexuality and destroyed the solid ground of definitions of obscenity and pornography; all of the many censorings and prosecutions of Genet's work, particularly in the USA, revealed the oppressive structures of power in the institutions and governments that attempted to impose those controls, rendering them exposed to ridicule and contestation. Genet's own position towards the suppression of his work exasperated those censoring bodies; supremely oblivious (he had, after all, originally desired that his work should be viewed as pornographic and be consumed as an obscene incitation, by himself first of all), he could summon up only a blasé contempt for the prosecutors of his work. Genet's obscenity is liberatory, or corrosively interrogates and overturns systems of power; his pornography constitutes a matter of the body in its perpetual confrontations with social order.

The penis forms a pre-eminent presence in Genet's novels; it is always vast in size (in the first, clandestine editions of the novels, the characters are often introduced with the exact dimensions of their penises included) and weighty, revealing its presence behind the thick cloth of a uniform, suit or dress; it drips semen as it heads towards a mouth or anus, and ejaculates spectacularly. It is the glorious presence that consolidates criminality or peripherality, always erect when a crime or act of treachery is about to take place; Genet releases his character's penises in the darkened zones of the city, under railway viaducts or in isolated public gardens overlooking the ocean. In the novels narrated by the figure of Genet himself, the penis is the supreme source of sensory elation, even when hidden; it obliterates all other concerns, and voraciously engulfs the world, capriciously obliterating it. By contrast, the anus is a far more sombre presence and the focus of desperate attention (in

Funeral Rites, the militiaman Riton, after days of being marooned on the rooftops of Paris, urgently attempts to clean his anus before being sodomized by the German soldiers accompanying him); it effusively expels blood, semen and excrement after its contact with the penis. Above all, the anus is an eye, itself multiply and panoramically aware of every nuance of action, and also the focus of vision, with all attention (both that of Genet's characters and readers) directed at that ocular core of sensation. Finally, in *Un Chant d'Amour*, without words, Genet demonstrates the image of the penis itself, meticulously selected (rather than film in close-up the penis of the man playing the older prisoner, Genet instead chose to use the immense penis of a theatre director, André Reybaz, who otherwise does not appear in the film); it delicately batters against the cell wall, which holds the eye of the hole through which the prisoners blow smoke, or else is simply gripped or masturbated in the hands of the other prisoners viewed by the guard through that other vulnerable eye of the spy hole.

Genet would discover new provocations and preoccupations in his subsequent work, after the years of silence precipitated, in part, by an exhaustion or over-accumulation of obscenity and its implications (profoundly inspirational for his readers, corrosive for Genet): in future writings, he would interrogate the human body in painting and sculpture, and the dynamics of power and representation in performance; ultimately, he would return to an incitation widely viewed as obscene in his political writings on terrorism. But even in that future work, where the immediate presence of the penis and the anus have vanished, they can momentarily force their way back into Genet's writings, such as in his essay on Rembrandt, with all of their overriding impact.

22

The Screens

In 1955, after several years of silence, Genet began a new phase in his work, pre-eminently with his first work on the writing of a vast spectacle of death, dreams and warfare, *The Screens*: it would evolve over the subsequent eleven years into a series of riotous, violent events with its first performances in France at the Odéon theatre. Genet worked on a number of other theatre works, both during the period when he was writing his novels and in the few years of the resurgence of his work from 1955, but it was in *The Screens* that he amassed his preoccupations with death, representation and the human body, generating them outwards from words and images into engulfing spectacles which he intended to form unique events, burning the perception both of his spectators and actors as his work itself vanished in its own conflagration. Contrary to theatre (Genet had no interest in any forms of performance other than his own, though elements of ancient Greek theatre resonate aberrantly in his projects), Genet's spectacles refused repetition and the illusory or placatory elements of representation; he intended his spectacles to be directed towards the world of the dead, from the origins of time. Genet's theatre works negate both the nature of theatre and the contemporary social world itself; to emphasize their intractable separation from all theatre and all societies, Genet planned to locate his spectacles in peripheral urban sites – *The Screens* was intended to be performed in a neglected or ruined cemetery, imbued with the presence of death and surmounted by the sexually resonant

The Odéon theatre, Paris, site of the demonstrations around the 1966 production of Genet's play *The Screens*.

shape of its crematorium chimney. However, for its charge of provocation to be fully unleashed, *The Screens* was ultimately performed in the very centre of Paris.

The Screens takes place in Algeria, in a moment of conflict: its characters must combat their grotesque colonial masters, their own wretched poverty, and their own responses to death itself – death forms both a desolate voice of horror, and an evanescent screen to be traversed in exhilaration and hilarity. The spectacle projects human figures who are all already dead or caught within death; all manifestations of perception are magnified to hallucination, or distorted into disorientated loss. Although *The Screens* possesses a deeply caustic view of colonial power (the time of the spectacle is able to encompass both the nineteenth-century French colonialization of Algeria and the contemporary moment itself, with the Algerian war of colonial liberation), its approach is oblique to that precise historical context. It dissolves history into flux in order to vastly expand its interrogation of death and into the impact it can exert on its spectator, who is forcibly displaced (temporarily, at least) into a terrain of death. In his notes accompanying the text of *The Screens*, Genet emphasized this uprooting of spectatorial perception through a confrontation with death: 'But the reader of these notes must not forget that the theatre where this work will be staged is constructed in a cemetery, that at this moment it's dark there and, somewhere, a dead body is being dug up to be reinterred elsewhere.'[22]

By the time that *The Screens* was performed in Paris, the entirety of the Algerian war (which was just beginning at the time Genet started work) had now elapsed; the loss of Algeria by the humiliated French had created fracture lines that would deepen over the subsequent decades, despite the concerted attempt by successive French governments to cast the entire conflict into oblivion. In 1966, at the time of the Odéon performances, the residue of the war was still a matter of raw fury for extreme right-wing organizations of former soldiers, who wanted the conflict to be reactivated or, at least, retrospectively glorified. *The Screens*, with its portrayal of the French colonial forces as imbecilic (their national identity articulated only via bouts of flatulence), provoked those organizations into action, particularly since Genet's spectacles were taking place in a prestigious national theatre. Genet himself had embedded that provocation both within his text and in the instructions he transmitted to his director, Roger Blin (who had also closely collaborated with Antonin Artaud). He exacted that the spectacle itself had to be rigorous: 'It will be extremely precise. Absolutely compact. No extraneous gestures. Every gesture must be *visible*.' But at the same time, he promoted an utter freedom for disorder among the spectators; they had the right to walk around the auditorium at will and approach the spectacle, and all manifestations of noise and all styles of behaviour and dress were allowed: 'The audience has the right to be mad.'[23] Throughout the series of performances, groups of irate protesters gathered in the street outside the Odéon and riotously stormed the theatre, held back by the police; inside the theatre, parachutists jumped down from the balcony and assaulted the stage area, while other protesters chanted insults at Genet and sang nationalistic songs. Genet remained in the Odéon throughout the spectacles, watching the riots with delight.

23

Unrest in the Theatre

The Screens was Genet's last-completed theatre work, and his final large-scale project until *A Loving Captive*, written in the period shortly before his death. But Genet's theatre projects had also extended throughout the early phases of his work, largely in the shadow of his novels; it was not until 1955, when Genet emerged from his long period of silence, that his experiments in performance briefly became pre-eminent in his work. By that time, Genet had definitively ceased working in fiction, and those theatre experiments served to concentrate down the livid extravagance of his novels into seminal preoccupations with the nature and representation of power and artifice, with the mutability of history and its capacity for interrogation through corrosive acts and gestures, and with the all-consuming desire to imagine or reformulate death. Many of Genet's concerns in his theatre projects remained inflected by the obsessions of his fiction, particularly by the compulsion to use language to immerse and transform brutal or unbearable subject matters: to impose an insolent style upon intractable calamities. But both the sexual or pornographic charge of that fiction was now largely absent, together with the corporeal and vocal presence of Genet himself, tangibly present in his novels as he manipulated his characters into sexual constellations that gave them an aura of glory in abjection. All of Genet's theatre (*The Screens*, above all) forms the antithesis of theatre and the disassembly of the entirety of its elements: the audience, the forms of representation, and the insularity of its gestures. Like Artaud's 'Theatre of Cruelty' of the 1930s, Genet's theatre is conceived in contempt of the habitual perceptions of theatre, and as an assault on the spectator; but, unlike Artaud (who could rarely realize his theatre projects, whereas Genet's theatre works were performed worldwide during his lifetime), Genet ensured that his spectacular provocations in theatre entranced as well as attacked his audiences' eyes and senses.

In the plays he had written during the period in the 1940s, when he was also working on his novels and beginning to envisage film projects, Genet assembles compact groups of characters to anatomize in detail the preoccupations which his novels generate out to expansive dimensions. The play set in a prison cell, *Death Watch*, employs a vocal rhythm of imprecations and invocations to propel its three enclosed characters into the only act, that of murder, that can defuse their escalating sexual tension. In *The Maids*, Genet uses the same compacted environment to conjure the hatred and desire of two subjugated sisters, pinioned within the gestural rituals of their domestic service, towards their oblivious mistress; gradually, the sisters evolve an oppositional but covert set of gestures of their own to formulate an act of murder, which they plan to inflict on their mistress but ultimately turn on themselves. Genet emphasized in his notes for the project that he aimed 'to establish a kind of unrest in the audience'.[24] Nico Papatakis attempted to make a film from Genet's play but, faced with Genet's refusal, he turned in his film – *Les Abysses* of 1966 – to the actual murder (that undertaken by the Papin sisters, who also inspired Jacques Lacan) which had been Genet's principal source material for *The Maids*. In his other theatre work of that period, *Splendid's*, the pre-eminent preoccupation with treachery in Genet's novels is projected into the spectacle of a group of gangsters, holed-up in a luxury hotel after botching a kidnapping and now awaiting their imminent capture by the police; like a band of outlaws evoked by

Genet in *The Thief's Journal*, they finally decide to betray themselves and the courageous tenacity of their own criminal acts by surrendering in ignominy to the police, in one exceptional gesture of luxurious cowardice, which is itself overturned at the last moment. Genet capriciously renounced *Splendid's* and it was never performed during his lifetime, although the British theatre director Neil Bartlett translated and staged it at the Lyric Hammersmith theatre in London in 1995.

Genet's conception of the nature of performance had entirely shifted by the time that he returned to his theatre work in 1955; all four of his remaining theatre projects were begun in that year, and all of them excavate the raw ground of power, representation and death. Genet developed a strategy of giving grandiose, verbose dialogue to his characters to generate a provocative juncture with the violent subject-matters which they endlessly talked over and elided. In *The Blacks*, that determining void is the impact of colonial power; in order for that power to be negated by Genet's black characters, it must first be incorporated and expelled, pre-eminently within a ritualistic form. During the period when he was working on *The Blacks*, Genet was deeply impressed by the French documentary director Jean Rouch's 1954 film *The Master Madmen*, in which a group of West African workers in a British colony perform a violent ritual in caustic imitation of their colonial masters, propelling themselves into an exhilarated trance in which they tear apart and eat a dog; their colonial subjugation is overridden by the self-imposition of cruelty and momentary insanity. *The Blacks*, written before the African decolonializations of the late 1950s and early 1960s, incises the turmoil of that process in progress; the impact of the play would lead to the Black Panther party's appeal for Genet's participation in their action against North American society, fifteen years later. In *The Balcony*, Genet probed the spectacle of revolution and its rapport of complicity with systems of power; the play, set in a brothel in which the sexual acts intricately double the gestures of a revolution taking place in the city surrounding it, is consumed with the nature of representation: no act can ever be established as original and definitive, and even death itself is elatedly encompassed within that volatile, multiple flux. Genet noted that the project formed 'the glorification of the Image and the Reflection'.[25] His final play from 1955, *She*, also interrogates the power of representation, but is placed within an atmosphere of aberrant derision as it ridicules the figure of a Pope who is being photographed for the media; the Pope, ludicrously half-naked and pushed along on castors, is as entirely composed of artifice as the drag queens in *Our Lady of the Flowers*, but that artifice here forms a stultified emanation of power which can be combated only through a savage debasement and unscreening. The entirety of Genet's theatre forms an insurgent project which ultimately applies that same strategy of combat to the nature of theatre itself.

24

Genet's Fragments

After the burst of work around 1955 from which his second
sequence of theatre projects emerged, Genet again entered a long
period in which silence predominated, although he was almost
always active, travelling from city to city and preoccupied with
his lovers of those years, in particular the young tightrope-walker
Abdallah Bentaga. During that period, Genet's pre-eminent medium
in his work was that of the fragment: he wrote short, intensive texts
– from a few lines to a page or so at most – around a particular
subject matter, until the fragments gradually accumulated, inter-
locking with one another into an intricate textual architecture
which was almost always left open or abandoned. All of Genet's
writings of the second half of the 1950s (his texts on Rembrandt
and Giacometti, and on the spectacle of death in Abdallah
Bentaga's highwire act) took this form; by the end of that decade,
Genet's fragments had grown sparer and more disintegrated, and
they would not cohere again until the early 1980s, when Genet
began to trace in fragments his memories of the intervening
decades (his stays with Palestinian refugees and the Black Panther
party, above all), until they formed the vast assemblage of often-
contrary, resistant fragments that comprises Genet's last book,
A Loving Captive.

Genet's fragments took a number of forms. He worked within
the medium of the fragment with the awareness that it provided
his preoccupations (themselves often concerned with the abrupt-

Genet in Paris, 1956.

ness of visual and sensory revelations) with an articulatory lucidity that came from its density and the concentration of its textual elements; this kind of intentional fragmentation possessed the power to project an idea or image with shattering precision, like that contained by a cry or exclamation, though edged with the danger that such an impacted and volatile means of expression might become scrambled by an excess of its elements. The fragment in that form always exists on a boundary between clarity and chaos. Alternatively, some of Genet's fragments were generated by a process of desperation, in which they took the form of all that which could be articulated or salvaged from a more wide-ranging interrogation of a subject-matter that had defeated or subjugated its author; this was often the case with Genet's writings at that time on death and the human figure. The fragment is then the debris (none the less potentially forceful and insightful for its raw state) that subsists from an encompassing project which has collapsed, often instigating a sense of despair in its author. This form of fragment parallels a figurative art, such as that of Francis Bacon, in which the human body can never be satisfactorily rendered in its entirety, and what emerge or are left from that vast work of representation are experiments and attempts, often pitched between intention, chance and desperation. Another form of Genet's fragment is that whose brevity and rawness are the result of its having been written at speed, in snatched moments of time between other activities; in the years after 1955, Genet was relentlessly travelling, on the move between hotel rooms across the world, and the process of writing became submerged into sudden bouts executed between predominating obsessions (such as his collaboration in designing Abdallah Bentaga's highwire act). The fragment then takes the form of the summary distillation of a far larger project which remained virtual: concertinaed in time to its essence in the fragment. The final form of Genet's fragment is the reverse of that previous form: it comprises the shreds or forgotten element of a larger project which the author wrote and even completed, but then destroyed; the few surviving fragments of Genet's text on Rembrandt are those which he neglected to tear up and flush down a toilet in 1964, in a period of anguish following the death of Abdallah Bentaga, which had engulfed his entire attitude to his writing. The fragment then takes a form independent of its author's desire to obliterate all of his texts; it is the separated element which escapes by chance from that wholesale erasure, and which its author then discovers or recuperates after he has calmed down, before making it publicly available as the surviving fragment of a destroyed work.

Genet made use, intentionally, of the fragment (like other writers and artists) to project his preoccupation in an essential, condensed form from which all extraneous elements had been subtracted; in Genet's work from the mid-1950s until the end of his life, the fragment pre-eminently seizes the human body and its perception in crisis. Above all, the fragment can extend that investigation infinitely across time, revealing insights that would be hidden or suppressed by narrative, anecdote or temporal fixity. Despite their spare, skeletal forms (like the sculptures of Giacometti), Genet's fragments are often as lavish and wildly vivid as the most elaborate passages of his early novels. But the fragment is also a dangerous medium: in Genet's work, it pivoted between language and its sudden loss into profound silence and desperation.

25

Rembrandt and the Wound

During the years 1957 and 1958, Genet travelled from city to city across Europe to see paintings by Rembrandt at the museums in which they were exhibited; occasionally making his visits coincide with productions of his plays in the same cities, he undertook journeys to Vienna, London, Munich, Amsterdam, Berlin and Dresden, assembling fragments in response to Rembrandt's work as his travels accumulated. Genet's fascination with Rembrandt's images worked to incorporate them within his preoccupations of that time with solitude and corporeal matter. In September 1958 the French newspaper *Le Monde* published several of Genet's fragments under the title 'The Secret of Rembrandt', as extracts from a forthcoming book. But the book never appeared and Genet never definitively ordered his fragments; the book project fell apart as Genet's silence deepened at the end of the 1950s, and the manuscript was then methodically torn into tiny squares of paper (over a period of several days) and destroyed in a hotel room in April 1964. Genet subsequently discovered two sequences of fragments that had accidentally escaped that destruction, and they were published in the review *Tel Quel* in 1967; finally, in 1995, those fragments were reunited with the material that had appeared in *Le Monde* and were published as a lavish volume, together with reproductions of the details of Rembrandt's paintings that are scrutinized in Genet's text. The resulting book constitutes an aberrant survival of Genet's Rembrandt text, put together in the face of his will to erase it, as the tenacious traces of an obliterated project.

Genet is overwhelmingly preoccupied with Rembrandt's paintings as physical emanations of disintegration that intimate a wound at the core of the human body. In Rembrandt's lifelong series of self-portraits, that determining wound becomes ever more apparent as the image increasingly intersects with death; the same process may also be at stake in a set of photographs taken of a human face, such as that of Genet himself, over a lifetime, although the tangibly worked material of paint can transmit the resonances of that process more directly. Genet goes straight to the heart of his obsessions in his engagement with Rembrandt; he is utterly disinterested in technique or skill of execution. Rembrandt's paintings undertake an unscreening and excoriation of the human body, to which Genet counterposes his own imagery of an all-encompassing wounding; pinpointing what he perceives to be the loving cruelty of Rembrandt's response to his elderly sitters in his portrait work, Genet notes:

> 'Here, decrepitude is no longer considered and applied as a picturesque element, but as something as lovable as absolutely anything else. Have you ever had a wound, on your elbow for instance, that has become inflamed? There is a crust there. With your fingernails, you lift it up. Underneath, the threads of pus which nourish that crust stretch back a long way. Without a doubt, the entire human organism is at work for the benefit of that crust.'[26]

Genet's reaction to that wound, on the body and in the material of the painting, is to conclude that every physical component, however infected or abject, possesses its own magnificence which, in turn, is exactly equal to that of every other element of the body: no element can ever be exempted from that engulfing cruelty of the painter's gaze, which simultaneously suffuses the body with an infinite validation and recognition. Genet perceives a gradual erasure of all human characteristics in Rembrandt's paintings, except for those which collect around that pivotal wounding; especially after the death of Rembrandt's wife, Saskia (whom Genet suspects to have been murdered by Rembrandt), the paintings are progressively stripped of their previous signs of wealth, vanity, dreams and contentment, until all that subsists is the spare, essential form: 'a figure reduced to the extreme, almost completely disappeared'.[27] That corporeal wound, able to 'salute' every other human form because of its absolute resemblance to them all, then vanishes into transparency.

In one of the sequences of fragments that Genet had intended to destroy, that concern with the mutability and identicality of human matter, always transmitted via the gaze, is extended into calamity through the form of a cursory narrative of a train journey. Rembrandt is absent, except for Genet's noting that the severity of the revelation he received during his journey corresponds to the severity of Rembrandt's own processes of corporeal revelation. Genet does not precisely situate his journey in time, although its geographical location (on the line between Salon and Saint-Rambert-d'Albon in southern France) suggests that it may have taken place during Genet's years as a soldier stationed in that region, over twenty years earlier. Catching the eye of the wretched, ugly man sitting opposite him in the carriage, Genet experiences their essential identicality as a movement of reciprocal flux between their gazes; contemplating the most dispossessed and disgusting human form, Genet is also gazing into his own face. That revelation – that all human identities are exactly equal to one another – forms an irreparable malediction for Genet, who connects his gaze at that infinite face with that of the vision of a pyramid of severed heads of sheep, piled up on the pavement of a streetmarket. If all physical identities and forms, however deviant or idiosyncratic, are reduced to that of only one human, who has become multiply fragmented into millions of temporary skin envelopes that are isolated from one another, this calamitous vision entails the extinguishment of all human rapports; above all, for Genet, that isolation and cancelled individuality impart the wrenching loss of the power of seduction. All that can save Genet and resuscitate the human body is the seminal and astonishing vision of a penis, which insurges suddenly into his text to combat his malign revelation in the railway carriage (whose transmission, from eye to eye, necessarily also incorporates and implicates the eye and gaze of Genet's own reader):

'An erect penis, heavy and vibrant with the flow of blood within it, sticking out from a mass of black curls of hair, then its continuation: the solid thighs, then the torso, the entire body, the hands, the thumbs, then the neck, the lips, the teeth, the nose, the hair, and finally the eyes which call out to future lovers, as though for rescue or for annihilation, and all that struggling against this fragile gaze which is capable, perhaps, of destroying the All-Powerful body?'[28]

26

Giacometti

During the same period when he was travelling around Europe
to view Rembrandt's paintings, Genet's close friendship with the
Swiss artist Alberto Giacometti was at its most intense phase:
Genet would declare at the end of his life that Giacometti had been
the only man he had ever admired. They met in the Saint-Germain-
des-Prés cafés and at Giacometti's cramped, dust-encrusted studio
in the backstreets of Montparnasse. Giacometti asked Genet to
pose for him, and Genet sat for over forty days on a wooden chair
in the studio while Giacometti executed several painted portraits
and innumerable drawings of Genet's figure, especially his head,
whose awry and rounded shape (and incipient baldness) fascinated
Giacometti. Although Genet was forbidden from smoking, he
could talk, and they conducted interrogative conversations in fragmentary bursts between Giacometti's extensive periods of totally
silent concentration. During the sittings and afterwards, to the end
of 1957, Genet assembled a text of fragments originating in those
exchanges and in his preoccupation with the rapport between
Giacometti's figures and death. Unlike his text on Rembrandt,
Genet's fragments on Giacometti were completed (or satisfactorily
abandoned, in suspension) and published, initially as a catalogue
text and then as a book interspersed with photographs, *The Studio
of Alberto Giacometti.*

All of the pivotal obsessions of Genet's fragments on Rembrandt
are also present in his writing about Giacometti: the wound, the

A sketch of Genet by Giacometti dated 1 September 1954.

Jean Genet by Alberto Giacometti (1954/5, oil on canvas).

disintegrating figure and the revelation of human identicality. But in the text on Giacometti, that sudden insight is projected wryly and attributed to Giacometti himself, who articulates it at the expense of Genet's vanity:

'I am seated, back straight, immobile, rigid (if I move, he rapidly returns me to order, to silence and stillness) on a very uncomfortable kitchen chair . . . HE (looking at me with an air of enchantment): "How beautiful you are." Then, he adds this statement, which enchants him even more: "Like everybody else, eh? Neither more, nor less."[29]

Genet possesses a neglected or subjugated presence in Giacometti's studio; unlike his novels and other writings, in which Genet and his self-generated glory form the absolute centre of attention, he is now peripheral to the action, chided and adroitly humbled by Giacometti's barbed asides, and centrally reconfigured only within the canvas upon which Giacometti works, which is itself a mass of erasures, cancelled gestures and marks that ultimately cohere around the gaze of the figure seized in the image. As in his Rembrandt fragments, Genet also highlights the abject, deteriorating human body and its personification in an elderly man whose identity engulfs every other: he evokes again the wretched figure of the old man sitting opposite him in the train between Salon and Saint-Rambert-d'Albon who provoked the recognition of human identicality also voiced, in astonishment, by Giacometti; later, he recounts his encounter in a café (while Giacometti sits impassively by, reading his newspaper) with a stuttering, drooling blind man, with whom Genet has a brief conversation on masturbation in the man's native Arabic language. Finally, Genet surmises that the blind man's principal characteristics – his anger and his vanishing into himself – only reinforce that identicality, which is both a malediction and the most precious element of life.

Genet examines the nature of the wound which he perceives as integral to the work both of Giacometti and of Rembrandt: the wound is not inflicted on the painting or sculpture, but every gesture irresistibly delineates and makes tangible that wound within the surface or material worked upon. In his Giacometti fragments, that realization of the wound undertaken by Giacometti has an illuminatory impact of beauty for Genet, rather than the revelation of cruelty that he received from Rembrandt's work:

> 'There is no other origin for beauty than the wound, which is dis-
> tinctive and different for every person, hidden or visible, which
> that person protects and preserves, and disappears into when
> they want to leave the world for a temporary but profound soli-
> tude . . . The art of Giacometti, it seems to me, seeks to discover
> that secret wound of every human being and even of every object,
> in order that that art may illuminate those beings and objects.'[30]

The disparity between Rembrandt and Giacometti in their rendering
of that wound is that while Rembrandt articulates it with infinite
slowness, in tension with death, over a lifetime of self-portraits,
Giacometti transmits it immediately, pre-eminently through the
gaze that moves with volatile speed between his own eyes, those of
his figures and those of Genet himself (and also those of all spectators
of Giacometti's work). Even Giacometti's own pulverized, dust-
engrained body emanates that wounding for Genet; for the rest
of his life, he would emulate Giacometti's self-immersal in an
exploratory abjection that precluded all elegance or social compromise (Genet would never again wear the ostentatious, expensive
suits of his first years of celebrity). In his subsequent years of
silence and disappearance, Genet would remain preoccupied with
the aura of death intimated by Giacometti's work, and with the
need to make discoveries in the most obscure or unforeseen places,
as he had done in Giacometti's studio:

> '(September 1957). The most beautiful sculpture of Giacometti
> (that done three years ago): I found it under the table, when I
> bent down to pick up a cigarette end. It was in the dust – he had
> hidden it, and the foot of a clumsy visitor could easily have
> broken it . . . HE: "If it is really strong, it will reveal itself, even
> if I hide it."'[31]

27

The Tightrope-Walker

Genet met the young circus performer Abdallah Bentaga in the
same year, 1955, that his work was briefly reactivated after years of
silence, generating his theatre projects and writings on Rembrandt
and Giacometti; Genet would declare at the end of his life that
Bentaga, along with Jean Decarnin, had been the most important
of his lovers. Bentaga, who was of mixed Algerian and German
parentage, was also Genet's first Muslim lover. He was twenty years
old and had been working in circuses since childhood, mainly
training horses. Genet's relationship with Bentaga determined the
course of the next nine years of his life: after 1957, Genet almost
entirely stopped writing and immersed himself in Bentaga's career.
He paid for Bentaga to have expert training as a tightrope-walker,
and involved himself both as Bentaga's manager and as the designer
of his act (Genet had always been fascinated by highwire spectacles)
– that act became ever more exacting and dangerous under Genet's
direction. His relationship with Bentaga also propelled Genet
into new travels following those he had undertaken to view
Rembrandt's paintings. Bentaga had been called-up for service as
a French soldier in the Algerian war (Algeria was then a French
colony, and officially part of France itself) and Genet persuaded
him to illegally escape his conscription; as a result, they could not
live in France, and began a long series of journeys over the next
years, to Greece, Denmark, Austria, Germany and Holland, living
in hotels in each city they traversed. While he trained Bentaga,

Genet conceived of vast writing projects to undertake in the future, particularly a project in many volumes to be entitled *Death*, but he wrote less and less as the years of their relationship went on, finally submerging into silence.

In March 1957, soon after Genet had decided that Bentaga should become an illustrious highwire artist, he wrote a short text of fragments in the form of an incitation addressed to Bentaga, *The Tightrope-Walker*. In this text Genet invests the entirety of the tightrope-walker's act with an aura of reverential glory that also envelops the astonished spectators who witness that act. Above all, Genet emphasizes the intimate rapport which the tightrope-walker must develop with the wire:

> 'This love – but almost desperate, but with a charge of tenderness – that you must show for your wire will possess as much strength as that shown by the wire in carrying you. I know about objects: their maliciousness, their cruelty, and their gratitude too. The wire was dead – or, if you prefer, mute and blind – until you appeared: now, it will live and speak.'[32]

Although Genet suffuses that rapport with tenderness, the view of the tightrope-walker's austere duty which encompasses it is deeply engrained with the imagery of death that is also present in Genet's writings on Rembrandt and Giacometti from the same period. The tightrope-walker works with Death (a distinctive, capitalized Death, separated from the more mundane death that surrounds his spectators) and incorporates death, both by rigorously contemplating death in preparation for his act, and then by forming the image of death during the act itself, which is executed with a calm awareness of the precipice on which the highwire artist stands and moves; that act forms an intricate dance of death for Genet – a dance in which the artist is always painfully aware of making gestures in tension with death (like those of the Japanese dance form 'Butoh'). Genet also stresses the wounding which he perceives as integral to the tightrope-walker's art, just as it is to that of Rembrandt and Giacometti (and to all human beings, animals and even objects) – in solitude before the crowd that awaits the moment of the fall into death, the highwire artist emanates an engulfing wound with each gesture. As with Genet's fragments on Rembrandt, an imagery of sex insurges into the text, aberrantly overturning its gravity: the tightrope-walker becomes an incandescent, walking erection from which 'a heat is disgorged that makes us glow'. But this transformation of the highwire artist into a glorious, vast penis is directed not towards the audience but towards the tightrope-walker himself: 'It's not a prostitute that we come to see at the circus: it's a solitary lover in pursuit of his image, who hides himself and loses consciousness on a wire of steel.'[33]

Genet places his own creative position into that of Abdallah Bentaga in his essay's final incitations:

'You are starting to show a great deal of talent, but it's certain that in a short time you will begin to despair of the wire, of your jumps, of the Circus and of your dance. You will experience a bitter period – a sort of Hell – and it will be after this crossing through a darkened forest that you will re-emerge, the master of your art . . . This is one of the most moving mysteries of all: after a period of brilliance, every artist enters a terrain of desperation, and risks losing his sanity and his mastery. But if he emerges victorious . . . '.[34]

Bentaga never re-emerged into the great triumph that Genet had envisaged for him: performing the act Genet had designed, he fell from the wire during a spectacle in Kuwait and badly injured his legs. Although he worked with Genet in Italy on resuscitating his act, his body had been irreparably impaired, and he could no longer walk on the highwire. Genet continued to travel with him for several years, but gradually transferred his attentions to promoting the racing-car career of Lucien Sénémaud's young step-son, Jacky Maglia; Genet began to follow Maglia to wherever he was living, initially to England, where Genet lived in a hotel in Norwich for many months. Abdallah Bentaga, now inactive, was abandoned by Genet in a small rented room in Paris, where he obsessively read Genet's books. In February 1964 he committed suicide by slashing his wrists and taking an overdose of Genet's sleeping pills. Genet was shattered: he travelled to Italy and destroyed his unpublished manuscripts in a hotel room, and told his friends he would never write again.

28

Death, Suicide, Silence

Shortly after meeting Abdallah Bentaga, Genet had conceived a vast project to be entitled *Death*, which would consolidate the momentum he had established with his work on his theatre projects of 1955, extending that creative furore by many years. In the subject matter of death, Genet believed he had both the means to revivify his work after the silence of the first half of the 1950s, and also the focus around which he could collect the preoccupations of his theatre projects within an all-engulfing, seminal obsession. By 1956, he already had an exact idea of the published form which *Death* would take. In an interview from that year, he announced:

> 'I'm going to write a great poem on death. A man like me sees death everywhere, he incessantly lives with death. It will be a book of great originality, printed on huge sheets of paper, at the centre of which there will be a number of small pages: a commentary on the main narrative, which will need to be read at the same time as that narrative. At the end, there will be a sort of lyrical explosion, which will also be entitled *Death*.'[35]

The project then expanded to even vaster dimensions, incorporating both a huge poem or prose narrative, *The Night*, and a sequence of seven interlinked theatre works. It would form an immense and challenging project to culminate Genet's work, demanding many years or decades to undertake. But Genet wrote almost nothing of

Genet in Florence, 1962.

Death: only a few scrambled fragments (although one of the envisaged theatre works, *The Screens*, separated itself from the project
and acquired an independent existence). Throughout the rest of his
life, Genet would be haunted by that unapproachable, lost project
which he had had the courage to conceive but not to execute. *Death*
survived in a handful of tattered pages of fragments, surrounded
by a profound silence.

In May 1967, three years after Bentaga's death, Genet himself
attempted to commit suicide in a hotel room in the Italian mountain
town of Domodossola, with an overdose of his sleeping tablets
combined with alcohol. He entered a coma and was taken to hospital,
but eventually reawakened and recovered. He had written nothing
for the previous decade, which he had spent in directing Bentaga's
circus career, then in despair at Bentaga's suicide: only the riots
around the Paris production of *The Screens* in the previous year had
broken that lassitude in momentary elation. He had been living in

Switzerland in a hotel in the centre of Geneva, but had crossed the border to Domodossola to commit suicide in anonymity and invisibility. After his release from the hospital, Genet took the train back to Paris. He would not attempt suicide again; when he discovered, twelve years later, that he had a potentially fatal throat cancer, he resisted death by every means and would tenaciously survive for a further seven years after his diagnosis.

Genet would maintain a silence in his creative work from 1958, when he finished the series of fragmentary texts on Rembrandt, Giacometti and the tightrope-walker, until 1983, when he began to write *A Loving Captive* – but it would be an idiosyncratic, often garrulous silence of twenty-five years' duration, encompassing the writing of many newspaper articles and outbursts of revolutionary provocation, within its overwhelming medium of a bleak, mute void: a refusal to speak as well as to write. The only momentum in his life was his increasing fury at social and political oppressions. Genet's silence itself possesses a life of its own and a tangible form: seething and screened from view, intermittently destroyed in public exclamations of condemnation, and stubbornly pursued in the face of Genet's worldwide celebrity of those decades. It is a silence that both awaits death, and simultaneously cancels death and all of its manifestations; it contrarily reinforces its own adamant strength by occasionally surrounding itself with a voluble outpouring of polemical denunciation, which vanishes as suddenly as it appears. And Genet's silence always existed only a paper-thin hotel wall away from the rest of the world.

29

Paule Thévenin and Genet

In 1965, the year following Abdallah Bentaga's suicide, Genet met the editor Paule Thévenin, whose fierce opposition to all social compromise and inflexible protection of Genet would make her the determining force in the political and revolutionary engagements of the final two decades of his life. Paule Thévenin, whose mother had been Algerian, was forty-three years old at the time; she had already spent almost twenty years editing the writings of Antonin Artaud, whom she had met in 1946 after Artaud's release from the asylum of Rodez (Artaud died two years later after collaborating closely with Paule Thévenin on his final radio projects, and left her an exacting lifetime of work by entrusting her with the publication of his *Collected Works*). Paule Thévenin met Genet in the offices of his publisher, Gallimard, and the theatre director Roger Blin (who had been a close friend of Artaud) then invited her to collaborate on preparing the text of Genet's *The Screens*, which he was about to stage at the Odéon theatre. Although Genet had fallen into a state of profound desperation and silence after Bentaga's suicide, Thévenin began to bring him back to life through a combination of sustaining attention and harsh incitation – she convinced Genet of the need to participate actively in combating social suppressions and acts of censorship, and constantly generated quarrels in which she and Genet angrily denounced people whom she accused of slighting or betraying Genet, such as Nico Papatakis. Thévenin's impact on Genet was

Genet photographed in Paris in 1963 by Henri Cartier-Bresson.

dynamic; he could not descend into lassitude or inaction once he was locked into his friendship with her, and for almost twenty years (cut by several periods in which their combative stance became directed at one another), Genet was impelled into radical political action and alliances of diverse, often contrary forms: first with the Black Panther party in the United States, then with the Palestinian refugees and terrorist organizations, and finally with the German Rote Armee Fraktion (Red Army Faction) terrorist movement. Although these engagements were interspersed with long periods of silence (Thévenin was never able to spur Genet into undertaking more than short articles or fragments), they ensured that Genet remained in a vital state of fury for the rest of his life.

In her uncompromising positions and acts, Thévenin embodied the insurgency of Artaud, who had written at the moment in 1948 when they were working in intimate collaboration:

'THE DUTY of the writer, of the poet, is not to cowardly shut himself away in a text, a book, a magazine, from which he will never emerge, but on the contrary to emerge, go outside, to shake, to attack the mind of the public: if not, what use is he?'³⁶

To that ferocious will to assault an audience (which Artaud conceived of as entailing a corporeal revolution rather than specifically political acts), Thévenin added her own radical preoccupations in the context of the turmoil of the late 1960s, with the period's worldwide uprisings and street riots against oppressive political regimes and military powers; although she was not a member of the French Communist party, Thévenin moved Genet towards extreme, confrontational action which embraced the use of violence as a strategy of liberation for subjugated individuals or groups. Above all, Thévenin infused Genet with her conviction that it was necessary to be perpetually alert to all compromise: Genet's life throughout his final years was impelled by an austere rigour and self-challenge in which even the least weakness in his approach to society had to be erased. The fidelity this entailed, manifested in escalating social provocations, formed the inverse quality to the treachery and self-betrayal that had underpinned the earlier decades of Genet's life.

But despite that strong fidelity (shown by Thévenin towards Genet in the form of endless hours devoted to looking after him and preparing his manuscripts for publication), a core of betrayal subsisted in Genet, and he abruptly terminated their friendship in 1984 with cruelty. Thévenin had become too essential to him and had witnessed his most vulnerable silences – she had accompanied him back to Paris after his 1967 suicide attempt – for him not to exact a final separation and betrayal. After Genet's death, Thévenin remained as unremittingly uncompromising as ever, though she allowed herself an aberrant moment of betrayal of her own when she came to speak of Genet in public:

'Clearly, in betraying him, I am faithful to him. But I find that wretched: it lacks any vivacity. This is not the elegance of Genet's treachery. He has burst through the white screen of paper into death and we are all still here on this side.'[37]

At her own death in 1993, Thévenin maintained her absolute fidelity to Genet; as she died, she kept on the bare wall by her bedside a tiny drawing by Roger Blin from Genet's *The Screens*.

30

Genet in Japan

In December 1967, seven months after his suicide attempt in Domodossola, Genet flew to Japan, where Jacky Maglia had gone to live with his Japanese wife. The journey was experienced by Genet as an intensely liberating experience and as an ecstatic separation from Europe, encapsulated in a single word of farewell articulated by the aeroplane's stewardess. Genet remained in Tokyo for several weeks, and would travel through India and Egypt (one of the projected destinations of his very first headlong flights as a child, from the Ecole Alembert in 1924) on his return journey. In escaping to Japan, Genet immersed himself in a world that he believed more exactly accorded with his own preoccupations with death and sexual transformation than Europe. He became fascinated with the Japanese Obon festival (although he did not witness it during his visit), in which the dead are honoured as lost but intimate presences by the living; corporeally void, the dead still maintain their existence, only a fragile membrane away from the places and people they knew during their lives. Along with that invocation of the dead by the living, Genet was also attracted by the Noh theatre with its own momentary apparitions of the dead, its wrenching mutations from one sex to another, and by its vocal acrobatics and sudden gestures.

At the time when Genet visited Japan, his reputation and influence there were immense. Genet was among the most inspirational and significant European cultural figures for Japanese writers, film-makers, choreographers and artists. From the end of the 1950s, with the translations of his novels into Japanese, Genet had become a seminal, revered presence in Japan, incessantly cited in the titles of art works and films. The director Nagisa Oshima drew his 1969 film *Journal of a Shinjuku Thief* (Shinjuku was the Tokyo district associated with experiments in art and the primary site of the city's anti-governmental riots) from Genet's *The Thief's Journal*, intercutting scenes of violent social protest with a fragmentary narrative about a book thief – who steals copies of Genet's books – and his exploration of criminality and sexual oscillation; Oshima cuts off his film with images of the devastation by rioters of Shinjuku police stations. In the same year, Toshio Matsumoto made his film *Funeral Parade of Roses* (a title compacting elements from several of Genet's works), which is set in a transvestites' bar called 'The Genet'. The first Japanese film to represent transvestite culture with approval, *Funeral Parade of Roses* is immersed in imageries of death, from scenes shot in a cemetery submerging underwater to sequences of murder, suicide and self-laceration. In its explicit scenes of sodomy and exhilarated group sex, counter-posed with the same kind of documentary images of street riots used by Oshima, the film manifests an exhaustive provocation which Japanese film-makers believed that Genet's work both incited and justified. The Japanese artist whose engagement with Genet proved to be most enduringly influential, the choreographer Tatsumi Hijikata, already had a longstanding admiration for Genet's work at the time of Oshima and Matsumoto's films; he had written a Genet-inspired manifesto at the end of the previous decade, *To Prison* (the imagery of a self-willed incarceration and of a deviant, sexually-imbued criminality formed a supreme provo-cation in the Japan of that era), and undertook a Tokyo street performance in 1961 of Genet's *Our Lady of the Flowers*, with his collaborator Kazuo Ohno in the role of Divine. Hijikata's dance style 'Butoh', which generated a huge international influence on choreography and art over the subsequent decades, vitally based itself upon the resistance, darkness and corporeal violence of Genet's writings, and on their imageries of glorious, painful transformation exacted in the face of social power and suppressions.

Despite the attempts by Tokyo's artists and writers to contact him during his visit to Japan, Genet remained utterly indifferent, preferring to spend his time with Jacky Maglia, who was involved in the Japanese militant protests against the ongoing Vietnam War (Japan had been occupied for seven years after the Second World War by American forces, who still maintained considerable influence in Japanese political life; the usa's air bases in the region of Tokyo were being used to supply its troops in Vietnam). In November 1969, at the time of the most fierce street riots between militant students and police in the avenues of Shinjuku, Genet returned for a second visit to Tokyo. On 17 December, along with Jacky Maglia, he attended a demonstration against the Vietnam War, ostentatiously taunting the line of riot-police drawn up in front of the demonstrators, at a moment of great tension. Several days after that single participation in Tokyo's spectacular urban affrontments, Genet left Japan and flew back to Paris; he never returned.

31

Genet and the Destruction of America

Between his two visits to Japan in 1967 and 1969, Genet travelled for the first time to the United States and witnessed the urban uproar that was detonating there, generated by many of the same factors as Tokyo's unrest: above all, the US intervention in South-East Asia, and the brutal arrogance of governmental power. On both of his visits to the United States, in 1968 and then in 1970, Genet had to enter the country clandestinely, having been refused a visa as a sexual pervert. From 1968, Genet began to write a great deal of political journalism and polemic, much of it under the instigation of Paule Thévenin. In France, Genet would write principally for the left-wing newspaper *L'Humanité*, but his first visit to the United States had its origin in a commission from a very different publication: the fashionable, mass-circulation American magazine *Esquire*. Genet agreed to write a reportage on the August 1968 Democratic Party Convention in Chicago, on the understanding that *Esquire* would also subsequently publish an article by him on the Vietnam War. In Chicago, Genet immersed himself in the protests (less violent and more idealistic than those staged by the Tokyo student movements) surrounding the Convention, and scrutinized both the police and the young pro-testers; in the company of the writers Allen Ginsberg and William Burroughs, he was soaked by water-cannons and chased by truncheon-wielding police of both sexes. Genet paid tribute to those police in his article (just as he had lauded the despised French militia in *Funeral Rites*): he wrote of the 'magnificent, divine, athletic' police

Genet in America, 1968.

who displayed the thighs of boxers or fighters as they frenziedly assaulted the largely peaceful crowd; the police were 'gorged with LSD, with rage and patriotism'.[38] Genet had formed an unremittingly negative view of the United States' system of power and its readiness to arbitrarily crush other countries, although he had a deep sympathy for its naïve young protesters; in the context of a magazine read by the governmental and social élites of the United States, he wrote with intense provocation: 'America is a weighty island: too weighty. It would be a good thing, for America and for the whole world, for it to be destroyed – for it to be reduced down to a fine powder.'[39] Genet extended his provocations into the domains of sex and death in his subsequent article on the Vietnam War, 'A Salute to the Hundred

Genet at the Chicago Democratic Convention, 1968.

Thousand Stars', in which he wrote with profound contempt, inflected with notes of amusement and incredulity, of the 'longest safari of the century' undertaken by the US soldiers in Vietnam:

> 'They fuck the prostitutes of Saigon, both the male and female prostitutes, they get robbed of their dollars and, when they have been killed but are still in one piece, they gladly allow themselves to be sodomized – or, if they are captured alive, they experience the most astonishing adventures.'[40]

Genet evokes with delight the vast numbers of young American penises severed by the soldiers' Communist adversaries. His article sent the editorship of *Esquire* into apoplexy and (to Genet's own fury) they refused to publish it.

Nearly two years later, in March 1970, Genet was invited to return to the United States by the Black Panther party, which had terrified and enraged the American government (and much of its white population) with its high profile demands for armed resistance to be exacted against the racist, militaristic power structures that kept the black population in subjugated poverty, and had dispatched many thousands of its young men to be slaughtered in Vietnam. Genet was attracted by the confrontational visual style of the Black Panthers, with their black leather jackets, extravagant hair and prominent weaponry; many of their leaders were already imprisoned, with little prospect of release. Although the Black Panthers who approached Genet in Paris were seeking his help in Europe (as the celebrated author of a play entitled *The Blacks*, who could intermediate for them with white intellectuals and raise funds), Genet immediately decided that he wanted to participate in the Black Panthers' acts in the United States, and left within days, crossing the border covertly via Canada, in the company of Jacky Maglia. The Black Panthers were eager for Genet to sway white students in their favour, and he conducted a speaking tour of university campuses, refusing the insistent

Genet, Jane Fonda and Raymond Masai Hewitt of the Black Panthers, 1968.

requests of the university authorities that he should also discuss his own literary work. At the largest spectacle, on 1 May at Yale University in New Haven, where Genet gave a speech as part of an open-air event spanning several days, a crowd of almost thirty thousand listened to him; unable to speak English more than haltingly, Genet pronounced the first words of his speech in French before allowing the Black Panthers' Minister of Information to read a translation on his behalf. Genet related the Black Panthers' struggle to the events of May 1968 in Paris, when vast groups of students had rioted, destabilized the government and attempted to create alliances with factory workers; Genet warned his audience that that insurgency had been dissipated by reactionary governmental forces. He distanced himself to some degree from the Black Panthers' disciplined objectives and increasing legal preoccupations, emphasizing his own status as a vagabond and sexual deviant with no regard for the law. He justified the Black Panthers' arrogance as a necessary response to the cold arrogance of American governmental power, and approved

Genet, Shirley Sutherland and Raymond Masai Hewitt with a Black Panther poster, 1968.

the Black Panthers' vilification of that power as 'fascist', arguing that any regime that was authoritarian, dominating and determined to violently intervene in other countries' affairs merited such an accusation. Finally, he instructed his audience of students that the revolutionary culture of the Black Panthers superseded, and should take precedence for them over their own university studies.

Genet left the United States on the day following his Yale appearance, threatened with arrest for entering the country illegally. But he remained engaged with the Black Panthers over the following years; in July 1970 he wrote an Introduction to the prison letters of George Jackson, a Black Panther supporter who had been imprisoned

Genet with Michel Foucault at a demonstration in Paris, 1972.

since the age of seventeen, and used the medium of the letter to articulate his uncompromising resistance and anger. In his Introduction, Genet declared his solidarity with all those who had written in conditions of incarceration (whether in prison, such as Jackson and the Marquis de Sade, or in asylums, such as Artaud). After Jackson had been gunned down by guards at San Quentin prison in August 1971, Genet wrote:

'It is more and more rare in Europe for a man to accept being killed for the ideas he believes in. The Blacks in America do this every day. For them, "liberty or death" is not an empty slogan. In joining the Black Panther party, all Blacks know they will be killed or will die in prison.'[41]

Into the mid-1970s, Genet supported the Communist activist and university professor Angela Davis, who had been imprisoned for alleged complicity with the Black Panthers' acts of violence and eventually released (he had feared she would share Jackson's fate).

Genet at the same Paris demonstration.

But Genet watched with wry detachment as the Black Panther party, after its sudden ascendancy, rapidly disintegrated in greed, drugs, compromise and media celebrity; he regarded its impact as that of a unique, unrepeatable moment of conflagration for the United States. Genet's involvement with the penal incarceration of Black Panther activists had its consequences in his subsequent engagements in France; he allied himself with the philosopher and prison reformer Michel Foucault in his organization's street demonstrations, staged to protest against prison conditions and the treatment of North African immigrant workers in France.

32

The Palestinians: Love and Death

Four months after his abrupt departure from the United States, Genet again set out on a journey of solidarity for a group of people whom he perceived as isolated within a hostile, crushing environment towards which they could exact a survival only by violent means: the Palestinians. As with his support of the Black Panther party, Genet conceived of his alliance with the Palestinians as being directed towards a peripheral, excluded body which accorded, however obliquely, with his own degraded and abjected position. The Palestinians had left the territory which became that of Israel in 1948; the hundreds of thousands of refugees who settled in camps in the adjoining country of Jordan were then joined by many more after the seizure of further territory by Israel in the Six Day War of 1967. The tensions between the Palestinians and the Jordanian military forces then erupted in violence in September 1970, and many of the Palestinians were confined to camps in a narrow strip of land on the Jordanian border with Israel (others left for the Lebanon and Syria); the Palestine Liberation Organization, led by Yasser Arafat, co-ordinated worldwide action – ranging from media spectacles to terrorist acts – to bring the population's endangered situation to prominence. Genet arrived in the Palestinian camps in the autumn of 1970, having travelled via Beirut and the Jordanian capital, Amman. He briefly met Arafat, who suggested that Genet should write a book on the Palestinian struggle (although Genet made no notes during his time in the camps), and gave him

Genet in a Palestinian refugee camp in Jordan, 1971.

a pass that enabled him to travel at will in the areas under Palestinian control. Having planned to spend only a few days in the camps, Genet remained there for the entire winter, returning to Paris only in April 1971: he slept in the collective tents of the young Palestinian fighters (who regularly vanished to undertake missions against targets both in Israel and Jordan) or in the open air. Genet experienced his stay with the Palestinians as one of great elation and friendship, compounded by the incessant proximity of death, since the camps were always under threat of being razed and the fighters massacred; for Genet, that confrontation with death generated a joyful fearlessness and created intense bonds between himself and the Palestinians. He would be haunted above all in the coming years by his momentary encounter with a young fighter named Hamza and his mother, with whom he stayed for one night in conditions of extreme danger.

Genet made three more visits to the region in 1971 and 1972, but on his third visit he realized he was under surveillance by the Jordanian police; concerned not to compromise his Palestinian friends, he left Amman immediately and did not return for over ten years. He was not the only writer or artist to visit the Palestinian camps; an incessant flow of visitors arrived from Europe, Japan and the United States, attempting to explore links between their own preoccupations with revolutionary action and those of the Palestinians. But Genet was an especially revered presence in the camps, able to communicate his empathy in simple gestures of friendship and alliance; his lengthy stay with the Palestinians and his own indifference to danger also articulated his profound commitment to them (as always, inflected with sexual preoccupations, directed towards the young fighters). Genet attempted many times over the subsequent years to write the book Arafat had suggested, eventually beginning the project that would become *A Loving Captive* in June 1983; in July of the following year, he finally returned to the now-transformed camps, searching for traces of the young fighter Hamza, whom he finally discovered living in exile in Germany.

The event which enabled Genet to begin work on *A Loving Captive*, after numerous misfired attempts, was a massacre: that of the Shatila refugee camp in Beirut, whose aftermath Genet witnessed in September 1982. His experience at Shatila unleashed a final burst of work after the accumulation of a silence of twenty-five years (intercut only by occasional articles and protests). Genet was ill and desperate, and had been abandoning project after project in Paris when his friend Leila Shahid told him she was about to leave for Beirut; she was a European representative of the PLO, and was concerned about the situation in the Lebanon, from where many Palestinian political figures were being expelled to Algeria, Tunisia and the Yemen. The Palestinian refugees in the Lebanon, housed in camps in the suburbs of Beirut since the late 1940s, were also under threat. Genet immediately decided that he wanted to accompany Leila Shahid, and they arrived in Beirut on 12 September. The city then underwent a sequence of upheavals, as though

Genet's presence itself had provoked them: the new President, Bechir Gemayal, was assassinated on 14 September, the Israeli army entered the city under the direction of Ariel Sharon on the following day, then rapidly surrounded the refugee camps of Shatila and Sabra. On 16 September the Lebanese Christian militia entered the camps with the complicity of the Israeli forces and massacred their populations. Genet was able to witness the situation in the Shatila camp on 19 September, before it was bulldozed and vanished. He posed as a journalist and spent four hours among the dense alleyways and shacks, where hundreds of the tortured corpses of the camp's inhabitants still lay in the positions in which they had been killed. After two days shut up in his room, Genet abruptly returned to Paris and spent the month of October writing a text, 'Four Hours at Shatila', for *La Revue d'études palestiniennes*. The text was written in a frenzy of exhilaration and rage; Genet had been propelled back into his creative obsessions. He wrote of how the massacred bodies had been heaped up as though, in their decomposition, they were engaged in sexual acts; he evoked the drunken cruelty of the militia as they cursed, danced, tortured and gouged out the eyes of their victims, as though enacting a vast spectacle of murder. Genet's deep empathy for the Palestinians was compacted both into his horror and into the resurgence of his creative work. He wrote: 'Love and death. These two terms fit together very quickly when one of them is written down. It was necessary for me to go to Shatila in order to be able to perceive the obscenity of love and the obscenity of death.'[42] Genet felt that his own body itself was now exuding death.

33

The Brutal Gesture

Before his journey to Shatila, Genet had instigated the last of his
three allegiances to peripheral groups, with his support for the
German Rote Armee Fraktion terrorist movement; this allegiance
involved the most explicit exploration of the rapport between violence and society undertaken by Genet, and led to his being virulently
attacked and condemned in the French media. Whereas the
Palestinian victims at Shatila would be the recipients of violence,
the RAF perpetrated violence as a revolutionary strategy, singling
out West German industrialists and politicians for assassination
(together with the policemen and chauffeurs who got in the way).
The RAF had links – albeit strained ones – with the Palestinians,
thereby ensuring Genet's support. Although Jean-Paul Sartre
had visited the group's leaders, who had all been imprisoned,
only Genet voiced outright support for them. Along with Paule
Thévenin (who was ambivalent about the terrorists, since they
were often from wealthy rather than oppressed origins), Genet
met many members of the RAF in Paris, and befriended one of
their lawyers, Klaus Croissant, in 1976. He was asked to write an
Introduction to the writings and prison letters of the terrorists'
leader Andreas Baader (as he had for George Jackson), and an
extract was published as an article on the front page of the newspaper *Le Monde* on 2 September 1977. Three days later, the RAF
kidnapped and eventually killed the West German industrialist
Hanns-Martin Schleyer. On 17 October 1977, the group's three

imprisoned leaders – Baader, Gudrun Ensslin and Jan-Karl Raspe – were found hanged in their solitary confinement cells; although they appeared to have committed suicide, many of their supporters believed that, along with Ulrike Meinhof in the previous year, they had been strangled by the prison authorities. Without its leaders, and in the face of concerted action by the West German police to crush it, the RAF fell apart at the end of the 1970s.

Genet's article in *Le Monde* was titled 'Violence and Brutality'. Genet made a distinction between salutary violence – that of the RAF, which was determined, directed at specific targets in West German corporate, political and military domains, and conceived as part of the revolutionary liberation of oppressed groups internationally – and reprehensible brutality, which was the mass, arbitrary subjugation enacted by regimes of dominating power, especially those of Western Europe and the United States. The Soviet Union was exempt from Genet's condemnations, since it was then offering its support to the Palestinians and therefore not 'brutal' (despite its many millions of labour-camp victims). For Genet, the RAF operates within an ultimate state of freedom generated by its violent resistance to society; its leaders' incarceration itself constitutes an act of social brutality: 'The brutal gesture is the gesture which breaks a free act.'[43] A barrier of purity exists between the RAF and its enemies, so that the terrorists are never contaminated in their revolutionary determination by the brutality (also pure) which saturates and delimits those enemies: 'But never, in all that I know of them, have the members of the RAF allowed their violence to become pure brutality, because they know that they would then be immediately transformed into the enemy they are fighting against.'[44] Genet's re-creation of the terrorists' chaotic confrontation with corporate bodies as a battle between two intractable purities would dissolve in the following month's media coverage and its bleak images of the terrorists' garrotted, convulsed corpses. But for several days after his article's publication, Genet faced a level of vitriol and exasperation he had never experienced before; this was exacerbated by denunciations of his article from Germany, where it had been published after Schleyer's kidnapping. The uproar silenced Genet completely for several years; unlike his writings on Shatila, which led on to the vaster project of *A Loving Captive*, his provocations on the RAF resulted only in a void.

The response to Genet's article indicated the rawness of the nerve he had touched in Europe. Very few writers and artists interrogated the languages, images and acts of West German terrorism; a prominent exception was the filmmaker Rainer Werner Fassbinder, with his film *The Third Generation* of 1979 and his contribution to the collective film *Germany in Autumn* of the previous year (although Fassbinder, unlike Genet, was by no means a supporter of the RAF). Several years later, in the spring of 1982, Fassbinder made the only film from Genet's fiction, metamorphosing *Querelle of Brest* into a hallucinatory projection of sexual duplicity and obsession. In his film, Fassbinder summarily compacted the novel's narrative elements and emphasized its awry distance between action and narration, thereby generating an impact of disorientated, fascinated participation for the film's spectators. Fassbinder wrote:

'*Querelle of Brest* by Jean Genet is perhaps the most radical novel in world literature, given its divergence between objective action and subjective imagination . . . What made it worth it for me was my confrontation with Jean Genet's mode of narration – a confrontation with an extraordinary imagination which generates for you a world that is daring from your first contact with it, a world that seems dominated by its own laws which emerge from an astonishing mythology.'[45]

Fassbinder died, aged only thirty-six, from an over-consumption of cocaine, immediately upon completing his film; Genet took no interest in the film, claiming he had now obliterated all memory of his novels, and did not see it, noting that he never went to the cinema because he could no longer smoke there.

34

A Loving Captive

Genet worked on his final book, *A Loving Captive*, for over two
years, from June 1983 to November 1985, in Morocco and Paris,
completing it only five months before his death. Activated by his
response to the Shatila massacre, the book had its origin in
imageries of death and moves towards death, gathering and juxta-
posing a multiplicity of languages and imageries of death as it
proceeds, unhurriedly, towards its extinguishment. A vast book,
A Loving Captive possesses no time or linear chronology as it collects
the memories of Genet's stay in the Palestinian camps and his
return journeys to the region: time itself is obliterated under the
force of memory, or concertinaed into dense, contrary intervals,
above all Genet's night spent at the house of the young fighter
Hamza and his mother, which provides the book's driving obsession
with the nature of memory, oblivion and death. Genet conceives
of his memory of that night as one of love, but it is a love (like
that experienced for the tortured, mutilated corpses of Shatila)
which integrally contains horror and obscenity: the flaws and
distortions of memory constitute an obscene act, just as the
exposed bodies caught and unscreened by memory, now aged or
tortured, carry the same charge of obscenity that captivates Genet.
The incarceration exacted by love, which confines Genet to the
enclosed Palestinian camps and then relentlessly pinions his memory,
directing it back towards the Palestinians, is enduringly allied
to Genet's penal incarcerations of forty years earlier, with their

Genet in the Théâtre des Amandiers, Nanterre, 1983.

adhesive sexual preoccupations: Genet remains liberated by the act of confinement.

In the first words of *A Loving Captive*, the urgent and uneasy gesture of initiating a language of memory is present:

> 'The page which was originally white is now traversed from top to bottom with minuscule black signs: letters, words, commas, exclamation marks, and it's thanks to them that this page is readable. But then comes a sort of disquiet of the spirit, a vertigo very close to nausea, a wavering which makes me hesitate to write: is reality this totality of black signs?'[46]

From that initiatory core of interrogation, Genet constructs his five hundred pages of fragments as a profoundly fragile but tenacious architecture of memory which heads towards its own vanishing. Although Genet's pre-eminent focus is on the Palestinians, he also allows his memories of the Black Panther party to insurge with violence into his book, though always immersed in a distanced irony which mocks the Panthers' frailties for greed and media celebrity; their revolution has itself become a media image, void of danger and banalized. But Genet also reserves a vast quantity of mockery for himself, castigating himself for his indelicacy towards the Palestinian fighters, who habitually indulge him with affection but occasionally transform Genet into an object of coruscating ridicule. Genet's friendships are always momentary and can be submerged instantly by death or anger. Wherever he travels in the Palestinian territory (whose interior is as dangerous and precarious as its borders), Genet comes face to face with the wounds of history, including his own memory of being a soldier in the region, four decades earlier; every elderly figure he encounters transmits both the abyss of history and the immediate moment of imminent death. All of the book's corporeal figures – both the joyful, doomed young terrorists and the old men who irresistibly project a history of

Genet at work in the Hôtel Sélecta, Paris, 1971.

death – gradually evanesce, along with Genet's own language, until only one memory, of the night spent with Hamza and his mother, survives to envelop all of the book's immense accumulation of marks and traces of love:

> 'I've done all I can to understand how this revolution was unlike others and in some ways I've understood, but what remains of it for me will be that little house in Irbid where I spent one night, and the fourteen years during which I tried to discover if that night really happened. This last page of my book is transparent.'[47]

Genet's book assembles his final fragments, intricately built to all-engulfing dimensions rather than pared to skeletal density as they had been in his writings on Giacometti and Rembrandt and on the figure of the tightrope-walker. Those fragments could have continued to expand endlessly, into an infinite book of death and memory; their point of termination was determined to some extent by the urgent factor of Genet's own imminent death, as the cancer he had had since 1979 reached its own terminal stage, and by his desire to see his book published before his death. Certainly, the ideal moment for the book to have materialized would have been at the exactly simultaneous moment as Genet's death; but the pages of ultimate black marks took their form a moment too late, appearing several weeks after that death.

35

Larache and London

In the final two years of his life, while writing *A Loving Captive*, Genet had been living in Morocco, in the city of Rabat and the Atlantic coastal town of Larache. He arranged for the construction of a house in Larache for his final lover, Mohammed El-Katrani, a drifter whom he had met in Tangiers, where El-Katrani had been sleeping on the pavement. During their relationship, El-Katrani had a son with a woman from whom he soon became estranged; Genet himself named the boy Azzedine, and became immensely attached to him. The house in Larache had a tree in its courtyard and was located close to the cliff-top cemetery where Genet would eventually be buried. Although a large upstairs room in the house was reserved for Genet, he preferred to stay in hotels until the very end of his life, and moved between a run-down hotel in the desolate centre of Larache and other hotels in Rabat, making friends with the desk-clerks and chambermaids. He also made visits to Paris to undergo therapy for his cancer, staying at hotels around the Place d'Italie so that he could easily reach by metro the hospital in the southern suburbs where he had his treatments; but ultimately, he abandoned those treatments.

In the final year of his life, Genet always needed money to give to Mohammed El-Katrani and to pay the fees for Azzedine's private school. In the summer of 1985, he was offered £10,000 in cash, in advance, to travel to London for an interview to be filmed over two days for the BBC arts programme *Arena*; Genet took the money, and arrived in London to give what would be his final interview. Genet, dressed in the casual and suave style of clothes he had worn since the 1950s, was driven to the house of the novelist Nigel Williams, who (apparently ill-prepared) conducted the interview in a state of terror, asking maladroit and directionless questions that rapidly exasperated Genet. He had been used in recent years to confronting and coolly taunting interviewers who possessed a comprehensive knowledge of his work and political alliances, such as the German novelist Hubert Fichte; but with Williams, Genet became angry at the blunt, opportunistic questions he faced: 'You're continuing to interrogate me exactly like the thief I was thirty years ago was interrogated by the police, by a squad of policemen.'[48] Contrarily, the banality of the questioning incited Genet into vivid evocations of his time at Mettray, and allowed him the liberty to shatter the structure of the interview, demanding that the BBC technicians usurp both himself and Williams from their positions of pre-eminence and authority. Genet's anger also enabled him to articulate a final, wry condemnation of society and its engulfing representations, which he had spent the last two decades of his life in uncompromisingly resisting: 'If at this moment my voice is breaking up, it's because I'm in the process of entering into normality, I'm in the process of entering into English family homes, and clearly I don't like that at all.'[49] Genet noted that the family constituted the first criminal cell in life: a crime that was exacted against the child. The interview tailed off with Williams attempting to wrest anecdotes about Genet's present activities in Morocco from him. Genet, implacable to the end, concluded by citing St Augustine: 'I am waiting for death.'[50]

After the BBC interview, Genet handed over the final manuscript of *A Loving Captive* for the publisher Gallimard to prepare for publication, and began a final journey with Jacky Maglia, travelling through Spain and to Morocco, where he saw Azzedine El-Katrani for the last time (Azzedine's father, Mohammed El-Katrani, would be killed in a car crash soon after Genet's own death). As he faced his imminent death in the spring of 1986, Genet continued to travel, stubbornly refusing to be fixed. He grew weak from the effects of his now-untreated cancer. Finally, he returned to Paris: the death he had so exhaustively anticipated and explored, over many decades, would abruptly seize him in that city.

36

Pages Torn from the Book of Genet

Genet's survival in contemporary Paris takes many forms, on the exterior facades of the city and within its interior spaces. After descending the stairs into the basement of the Institut Mémoire de l'Edition Contemporaine archives, the vault where Genet's manuscripts are kept appears: fluorescently illuminated, its air maintained at an even, cool temperature, that subterranean space exudes the calm power of death which Genet always interrogated and incessantly overturned. That power now has the upper hand. Along a side-chamber, roofed with brick arches, the grey metal cabinets that house Genet's notebooks and infinite sheets of handwritten pages hold their ground in Paris, as though substituting in their mass for Genet's own body, buried high above the ocean in Larache. Inside the cabinets, those manuscripts from every point of Genet's life carry the gestures of fury, sexual obsession and treachery – rarely over-written or effaced, imprinted rapidly on the page – that sent those writings into the outside world, into projects for creative uproar or revolutionary upheaval sparked by Genet's work: from Europe to East Asia, from North Africa to the United States. The vault also contains Genet's silence, embedded deeply within those manuscripts as an enduring laceration, or insurging in the form of a fragment inscribed in isolation within the void of otherwise untouched pages. Such an intrusion into that mass of pages damages Genet's silence: after you re-ascend the stairs and leave the vault, the body of Genet's manuscripts immediately seizes back its essential solitude.

At some point in the future, Genet's manuscripts will be digitalized and made instantaneously visible or exposed on any computer screen. But the evidence of corporeal traces, gestural striations and sheer speed or negation in those manuscripts exists in tension with that coming transformation, which will shatter their silence, space and time forever. The digital text or image, with its axis in its own always replicable and amendable status, overrules Genet's vision of unique criminal or creative acts that continue to resonate endlessly around the glorious bodies of their perpetrators: acts which disseminate their impact to the outside world aberrantly, in unforeseen deviations and sexual incitations that captivate or assault their readers and spectators. In their obstinacy, Genet's writings form an archaic resistance to the homogeneity of digital culture and its corporate imperatives; but those writings are simultaneously contemporary in their cross-media explorations of the body, of the extreme points of sex and language, of the exercise of oppressive power and subjugation (with its own obstinate sites of violence and repetition: the Middle East, above all), and in their movement – however calamitous – into revolution or death. The future digital book of Genet will be an integrally explosive object.

Out on the streets of contemporary Paris, the traces of Genet's life and obsessions are still tangible: the walls of the Santé prison still contain France's most notorious criminals, terrorists and legendary figures; the Tarnier clinic, where Genet was born as an unwanted bastard in 1910, maintains its embodiment of the city's cruel philanthropy; and Jack's Hotel, where Genet died as an anonymous customer in 1986, still keeps its down-market profile in the city's back-streets. Other seminal sites of Genet's life, such as the Petite-Roquette children's prison, have been destroyed or subsist only in fragments (the original gate of the Petite-Roquette, through which Genet entered as a recalcitrant fifteen-year-old, stands in isolation beside the public park that replaced the demolished prison). In the contemporary city – coursed more than ever by the forces of a system of social exclusion that Genet attacked, while embracing his own, self-generated social exclusion – the urban surfaces enduringly hold the peripheral traces of memory, of bodies, of languages and images, that tenaciously constitute Genet's survival.

References

1. *L'Ennemi Déclaré* (Paris, 1991), p. 223.
2. *Un Captif Amoureux* (Paris, 1986), p. 453.
3. Albert Dichy and Pascal Fouché, *Jean Genet: Essai de Chronologie 1910–1944* (Paris, 1988), p. 155.
4. *Ibid.*, p. 170.
5. *L'Ennemi Déclaré*, p. 233.
6. Dichy and Fouché, *Jean Genet: Essai de Chronologie*, p. 211.
7. *Notre-Dame-des-Fleurs* (Paris, 2001), pp. 106–7.
8. *Ibid.*, pp. 241–2.
9. *Miracle de la Rose* (Paris, 2000), p. 42.
10. *Ibid.*, p. 306.
11. *Pompes Funèbres* (Paris, 2000), pp. 157–8.
12. *Ibid.*, p. 202.
13. *Querelle de Brest* (Paris, 2001), p. 99.
14. *Ibid.*, p. 225.
15. *Journal du Voleur* (Paris, 2001), p. 84.
16. *Ibid.*, pp. 138–9.
17. *Le Monde*, newspaper (Paris, 12 May 1989), p. 22.
18. *Ibid.*, p. 22.
19. *Le Bagne* (Décines, 1994), p. 99.
20. *Ibid.*, p. 215.
21. François Sentein, *Nouvelles Minutes d'un Libertin* (Paris, 2000), p. 218.
22. *Les Paravents* (Paris, 1989), p. 93.

23. *Ibid.*, p. 10.
24. *Les Bonnes* (Décines, 1976), p. 10.
25. *Le Balcon* (Décines, 1983), p. 10.
26. *Rembrandt* (Paris, 1995), pp. 14–15.
27. *Ibid.*, p. 34.
28. *Ibid.*, pp. 62–3.
29. *L'Atelier d'Alberto Giacometti* (Décines, 1986), unpaginated.
30. *Ibid.*, unpaginated.
31. *Ibid.*, unpaginated.
32. *Le Funambule*, in *Oeuvres Complètes*, v (Paris, 1979), p. 9.
33. *Ibid.*, p. 19.
34. *Ibid.*, p. 26.
35. *Bulletin de Paris*, newspaper (19 July 1956), pp. 10–11.
36. Antonin Artaud, letter to René Guilly, in Artaud, *Oeuvres Complètes*, xiii (Paris, 1974), pp. 136–7.
37. *Le Monde* (12 May 1989), p. 22.
38. *L'Ennemi Déclaré*, pp. 312–3.
39. *Ibid.*, p. 318.
40. *Ibid.*, p. 322.
41. *Ibid.*, p. 111.
42. *Ibid.*, p. 245.
43. *Ibid.*, p. 200.
44. *Ibid.*, p. 201.
45. Rainer Werner Fassbinder, *Querelle Filmbuch* (Munich, 1982), p. 11.
46. *Un Captif Amoureux*, p. 11.
47. *Ibid.*, p. 504.
48. *L'Ennemi Déclaré*, p. 298.
49. *Ibid.*, p. 305.
50. *Ibid.*, p. 306.

Bibliography

1. Genet's books in French

The *Pléiade* (complete and authoritatively annotated) edition of Genet's theatrical works and writings was published by Gallimard in Paris in 2002, edited by Albert Dichy and Michel Corvin. Genet's writings exist in an *Oeuvres Complètes* edition in six volumes, also published by Gallimard, and also in inexpensive paperback editions published under the Folio and L'Imaginaire imprints. Other notable editions of Genet's writings are:

L'Atelier d'Alberto Giacometti (Décines, 1986)
Lettres à Olga et Marc Barbezat (Décines, 1989)
Lettres au Petit Franz (Paris, 2000)
Lettres à Roger Blin (Paris, 1986)
Rembrandt (Paris, 1995)

Two particularly valuable special-issues of journals have been devoted to Genet's work:
Magazine Littéraire, issue 313 (Paris, 1993)
Théâtres au Cinéma, issue 10 (Bobigny, 1999)

2. Genet's books in English

The Balcony, trans. Bernard Frechtman (London and New York, 1997)
The Blacks, trans. Bernard Frechtman (New York, 1988, London, 1989)
The Complete Poems, trans. Jeremy Reed (Maidstone UK, 2001)
Deathwatch, trans. Bernard Frechtman (London and New York, 1989)

Funeral Rites, trans. Bernard Frechtman (London, 1990, New York, 1997)
The Maids, trans. Bernard Frechtman (London and New York, 1989)
May Day Speech, trans. Richard Howard (San Francisco, 1970)
Miracle of the Rose, trans. Bernard Frechtman (New York, 1998, London, 2000)
Our Lady of the Flowers, trans. Bernard Frechtman (London, 1990, New York, 2001)
Prisoner of Love, trans. Barbara Bray (London, 1989, New York, 2003)
Querelle of Brest, trans. Gregory Streatham (London, 2000, New York, 2001)
Rembrandt, trans. Bernard Frechtman and Randolph Hough (New York, 1995)
The Screens, trans. Bernard Frechtman (London and New York, 2000)
The Selected Writings of Jean Genet (New York, 1995)
Splendid's, trans. Neil Bartlett (London, 1995)
The Thief's Journal, trans. Bernard Frechtman (New York, 1997, London, 2000)

3. Essential writings in English on Genet and his work

Choukri, Mohamed, *Jean Genet in Tangier* (New York, 1993)
Giles, Jane, *Criminal Desires: Jean Genet and Cinema* (London and New York, 2002)
Read, Barbara, ed., *Flowers and Revolution: A Collection of Writings on Jean Genet* (London, 1997)
White, Edmund, *Genet* (London and New York, 1993)

4. Genet's film work

Un Chant d'Amour was issued on video by the British Film Institute, London, in 1989. It was issued on DVD, again by the British Film Institute, in 2003.

Acknowledgements

For speaking to me about Genet and his work, I'd like to thank
Neil Bartlett, Tahar Ben Jelloun, Albert Dichy, Jane Giles,
Nico Papatakis, Leila Shahid, Patti Smith, Paule Thévenin
(who has since died), Kuniichi Uno and Edmund White.
I'm grateful to the Leverhulme Trust and to the Arts and
Humanities Research Board for the grants they awarded me
for my work on this book.

This book was researched at the IMEC archives in Paris.
All translations are my own.

Photographic Acknowledgements

The author and publishers wish to express their thanks to the below sources of illustrative material and/or permission to reproduce it:

Photo © ADAGP, Paris and DACS, London 2004: p. 103; photos by or courtesy of the author: pp. 13, 14, 21, 31, 87; photo © Bruno Barbey/Magnum Photos: p.130; photo Pierre Bourgeade, courtesy Galerie à l'Enseigne des Oudin, Paris: p. 140; photo © Henri Cartier-Bresson/Magnum Photos: p. 115; photo © Raymond Depardon/ Magnum Photos: p. 123; photo Fonds Jean Genet/Archives IMEC: p. 28; photo Globe Photos/Rex Features p. 126; photo Jacques Guérin: p. 80; photos Ken Howard/Rex Features: pp. 122, 125; Musée National d'Art Moderne, Paris: p. 59 (photo Hervé Landowski/RMN, © Estate Brassaï – RMN), 104 (photo Adam Rzepka/CNAC/MNAM Dist. RMN, © ADAGP, Paris and DACS, London 2004); photo © Rajak Ohanian/RAPHO: p. 138; photo Lutfi Özkök: p. 112; photo Roger Viollet/Rex Features: p. 61; photo Roger Parry/© Gallimard: p. 82; photos Sipa Press/Rex Features: pp. 112, 127, 128.